Searching for
Heaven
on
Earth
Journal

HOW TO FIND WHAT REALLY MATTERS IN LIFE

Searching for
Heaven
on
Earth
Journal

DAVID
JEREMIAH

INTEGRITY®
PUBLISHERS
Nashville

SEARCHING FOR HEAVEN ON EARTH JOURNAL

Copyright © 2004 David Jeremiah

Published by Integrity Publishers, a division of Integrity Media, Inc.,
5250 Virginia Way, Suite 110, Brentwood, TN 37027.

HELPING PEOPLE WORLDWIDE EXPERIENCE *the* MANIFEST PRESENCE
of GOD.

Published in association with Yates & Yates, LLP, Literary Agents, Orange, California.

Scripture quotations are taken from the New King James Version (NKJV®),
copyright © 1979, 1980, 1982, Thomas Nelson, Inc., Publishers.

Design: UDG | DesignWorks, www.udgdesignworks.com

ISBN 1-59145-221-X

Printed in the United States of America
04 05 06 07 08 09 PHX 9 8 7 6 5 4 3 2 1

Searching for Heaven on Earth Journal

CONTENTS

INTRODUCTION

⁓

As Dr. Jeremiah's publishers, we know *Searching for Heaven on Earth* has stirred your heart just as it did ours. It raised issues that made us want to respond—to talk, to write, to discuss, to reread our Bibles.

Some books need an outlet for the heart—and *Searching for Heaven on Earth* is one of them. As a result, we want to invite you to become a writer in the quietness of a reading moment by speaking through your pen.

You may already be an avid "journaler" who has discovered how to give voice to your heart by writing. If not, hopefully this journal will begin a lifelong practice of reflection and self-discovery as you express your beliefs, questions, decisions, dreams, wonderings, prayers.

Searching for Heaven on Earth has thirty-one chapters, and you will find a corresponding section in this journal for each chapter. In each journal section you'll be reminded of the passage in Ecclesiastes under consideration, a key verse to contemplate or memorize, and a quote from David Jeremiah that summarizes the chapter's message.

Then comes a series of quotes from the chapter and a brief comment or question encouraging you to respond from your heart to what you've read. At the end of each section is a place to reflect on your growth and an opportunity to call upon God in a way that is personal to you.

What you write in this journal won't be published, nor should it be. It's yours alone, as secret and personal as the heart from which it comes. But it's God's too. Thankfully, He knows our hearts, bottles up our tears, and reads our words with perfect understanding.

So write, won't you? And pray and reflect. May your search for heaven on earth find new expression through your prayers and your pen.

Journeying and journaling with you,

—THE PUBLISHERS

Day 1

WILL THE CIRCLE BE UNBROKEN?

DAILY READING: Ecclesiastes 1:1–7

KEY VERSE
"Vanity of vanities," says the Preacher. "Vanity of vanities, all is vanity." —Ecclesiastes 1:2

BIG IDEA
We were not created to live under the sun or over the rainbow, but above it all—
seated in Christ in heavenly places at the right hand of God.

—DAVID JEREMIAH

EXCURSION JOURNAL
Notice the phrase *under the sun*. This is another of those characteristic phrases to be
encountered nearly everywhere in this book—twenty-nine times in this case. *Under
the sun* implies an earthbound view of things. Solomon wasn't speaking from any
pious, eternal perspective. Remember, he had drifted away from his Lord over the
years—day by day, inch by inch, worldly entanglement by worldly entanglement.

*Reflect on your own experiences of vanity (meaninglessness) and dissatisfaction with an earth-
bound view of things:*

_____
_____
_____
_____
_____
_____

*Reflect also on your own conversation. How much is earth-centered and how much is
heaven-centered?*

_____
_____
_____
_____
_____

Solomon returns often to the subject of death. Remember, he's in the twilight of life and his spirits have withered. No wonder! When life is built without a spiritual foundation, death is a killer on the prowl, peering in at the window.

Bertrand Russell shares this same sense of despair when he writes in his autobiography, "We stand on the shore of an ocean, crying to the night and the emptiness; sometimes a voice answers out of the darkness. But it is the voice of one drowning, and in a moment the silence returns."

How does death preoccupy the life of the person who lives without a spiritual foundation?

_____

_____

_____

_____

_____

_____

We get up, go to work, come home, watch TV, go to bed—only to repeat until retirement. Then we die. Or at least that's how a lot of people view life.

Solomon is saying, "On the surface, life looks like a gerbil running on a wheel. What's the point?" At least, that's how it can look if you don't have eyes to see beneath the surface.

Consider what is beneath the surface of your life that keeps daily routines from becoming meaningless:

_____

_____

_____

_____

_____

_____

It's intriguing that Ernest Hemingway chose these words, *The Sun Also Rises*, as the title of his first best-selling novel. He wrote of "lost generation" Americans and Brits after the First World War, and his book conveys the despair that characterized his life and writings. Years later, shortly before his suicide, the great writer confessed, "I live in a vacuum that is as lonely as a radio tube when the batteries are dead and there is no current to plug into."

Reflect on the presence, or absence, of currents in your life:

_____

_____

_____

_____

_____

A psychologist named William Moulton Marston asked three thousand individuals, "What have you to live for?" The answers shocked him. He found that 94 percent were not living at all; they were simply enduring the present while waiting for something in the future. They were waiting for *something* to happen—waiting for children to grow up and leave home, waiting for next year when things would be better or at least different, waiting for the chance to take a trip, waiting for tomorrow. *Waiting . . . waiting.* For them, life had deteriorated to a cycle with little meaning in and of itself.

Contrast the degree to which your life is spent waiting or living:

_____

_____

_____

_____

_____

We all have an enduring sense that the universe got it wrong, that things are exactly the reverse of what they should be. Shouldn't the ignorant machine of nature be temporary, and *we* be permanent? We just know this somehow; as Solomon will soon tell us, we have eternity set in our hearts (3:11). We refuse to see ourselves as temporal creatures. We're made for everlasting life, and the clock we live on should run down while we go on forever.

But under-the-sun thinking keeps us from making the leap—from finding out that our intuition is exactly correct. The truth can't be found under the sun, but in the One who set it in motion and presides over it.

On the other hand, over-the-rainbow thinking is equally deceptive. Baseless optimism is one more dead-end street. We are to live not *under* or *over*— but above.

To what degree is your life being lived "under the sun"? Reflect on what life is like when lived "under heaven" instead:

_____

_____

_____

_____

_____

_____

_____

_____

_____

CHECKING YOUR PROGRESS
About what area of your life do you sometimes secretly wonder, "What's the point?"

_____

_____

_____

_____

_____

_____

_____

_____

_____

ASKING FOR DIRECTIONS
Write a prayer asking God to give you an illustration today of why that area of your life really does matter, why it's not meaningless. (Don't forget to come back and record what He shows you.)

_____

_____

_____

_____

_____

_____

_____

_____

_____

Day 2

BORED TO DEATH

KEY VERSE
Is there anything of which it may be said, "See, this is new"?
It has already been in ancient times before us. —Ecclesiastes 1:10

BIG IDEA
None but Christ can fill the God-shaped hole in the human heart, though men spend their lives trying every other possibility in vain. But the moment the rightful Lord of your soul fills its vacuum, there will be a fullness such as you never knew could be possible under the sun. —DAVID JEREMIAH

EXCURSION JOURNAL
Popular novelist Kathe Koja has claimed: "Everyone is cored by that existential void, the deep hole in the heart that cries for radiance; our entire consumer culture is predicated on the belief that, if you stuff enough things down that hole, you can finally satisfy it into silence. That has never been the case. Nor does creativity, sex, art, or even love fill that hole."

Reflect on the things you have used at various times to fill the "deep hole in the heart":

_____

_____

_____

_____

_____

_____

_____

The natural outgrowth of futility is frustration—or worse. All around us in our world we see frustrated people—road rage on the freeways, shooting sprees in corporate offices, hopelessness in the hearts of individuals. In his observations, Solomon moves from the evidence of futility to the evidence of frustration when God is removed from the picture.

How can you use frustration as a barometer in your life to measure your God-centeredness?

_____

_____

_____

_____

_____

"Boring!"—usually pronounced "Boooooo-rring!"—is the ultimate put-down in today's society, yet everyone and everything seems afflicted by it. Verse 8 explains why. Nothing "under the sun" satisfies. We can never see enough or hear enough to bring satisfaction. Everything ultimately brings weariness and boredom, forcing us to constantly seek diversion. Our entire entertainment industry rests on this premise.

Reflect on the difference between entertainment as a means to an end versus an end in itself. What role does entertainment play in your life?

_____

_____

_____

_____

_____

Michael Crichton's thriller *Timeline* has an interesting take on [life]. . . . : "In other centuries, human beings wanted to be saved, or improved, or freed, or educated. But in our century, they want to be entertained. The great fear is not of disease or death, but of boredom. A sense of time on our hands, a sense of nothing to do. A sense that we are not amused. But where will this mania for entertainment end?"

_____

_____

_____

_____

How is it possible to be busy and bored at the same time; to be busy but have nothing to do? What is the solution to this contradiction?

_____

_____

_____

_____

_____

In his profound book, *Man's Search for Meaning*, Victor Frankl wrote . . . : "Now we can understand Schopenhauer when he said that mankind was apparently doomed to vacillate eternally between the two extremes of distress and boredom. In actual fact, boredom is now causing, and certainly bringing psychiatrists, more problems to solve than distress. And these problems are growing increasingly crucial."

What are the evidences you see in our culture, in your own life, that the above statement is true?

_____

_____

_____

_____

_____

_____

We look at the world that is around us—what we can see and feel and hear, under the sun—and we realize there is nothing new. It is as it ever was. The old deist school of theology loved to set up the visual image this way: God was the great watchmaker who built a beautiful watch (the universe), and then just walked away, abandoning it to run forever. Nothing is new, just the same old tick-tick-ticking.

What evidence that the deist theology is wrong do you depend on in your life?

_____

_____

_____

_____

_____

God has made us in such a way that until we return home to the arms of our Father, we will be like the prodigal son [Luke 15:11–32], a miserable and misplaced heir to a lost kingdom.

Where are you in relationship to the arms of our Father?

_____

_____

_____

_____

_____

CHECKING YOUR PROGRESS

Briefly chronicle the story of your life in terms of what has filled the God-shaped vacuum in your heart:

_____

_____

_____

_____

_____

_____

_____

_____

_____

_____

_____

ASKING FOR DIRECTIONS

Turn Psalm 42:1 into a prayer, in your own words, asking God to be your ultimate source of satisfaction: "As the deer pants for the water brooks, so pants my soul for You, O God."

_____

_____

_____

_____

_____

_____

_____

_____

_____

_____

_____

Day 3

TRIVIAL PURSUITS

DAILY READING: Ecclesiastes 1:12–2:11

KEY VERSE

Then I looked on all the works that my hands had done and on the labor in which I had toiled; and indeed all was vanity and grasping for the wind. There was no profit under the sun.
—Ecclesiastes 2:11

BIG IDEA

Don't make the same timeless error that Solomon did. He sought meaning in things and experiences. He searched in wisdom, in wild living, in work, in wealth—in vain. The object of his search was, in fact, unavailable under the sun.
—DAVID JEREMIAH

EXCURSION JOURNAL

Solomon was confused. He pursued education, wisdom, and knowledge as no one before him had done. And the fuller his mastery of these fields, the emptier they seemed. "I perceived that this also is grasping for the wind," he concluded wearily. "For in much wisdom is much grief, and he who increases his knowledge, increases sorrow" (Ecclesiastes 1:17–18).

From your own experience, reflect on the accuracy of Solomon's statement:

_____

_____

_____

_____

_____

_____

For all its benefits, education and intellectual attainment can only speak to us about life under the sun. The rest of the story is found in God's revealed Word. When we neglect or reject the revealed truth of Scripture, even our most brilliant scientists and professors are little more than mice scurrying around inside a piano, analyzing all the hammers and strings, willfully ignorant of the musical score sitting on the stand above the keys.

Think about the difference in value you place on books versus the Book:

_____

_____

_____

_____

_____

"Even in laughter the heart may sorrow, and the end of mirth may be grief" (Proverbs 14:13). For many, laughter only breaks the monotony of crying, and pleasure is only an intermission to pain. Solomon was trying to be happy, but he was failing.

What role does pleasure play in your life—is it a form of medication or legitimate satisfaction?

_____

_____

_____

_____

_____

The bottomless budgets of the liquor industry make drinking seem very attractive today. A wine glass or beer bottle becomes a ticket to social acceptance for our young people, and soon they feel naked without it. Campus parties and social life revolve completely around drinking and intoxication, as if these were the most glorious of pursuits, the focus of life itself. Meanwhile, the mounting tragedies of drunk driving and dissipated lives are ignored, because who can shout over the message of movies, songs, and TV commercials that glorify the emptiness?

_____

_____

_____

_____

Remind yourself of the reasons you choose to abstain from or to partake of alcoholic beverages— and whether you are currently satisfied with your reasoning:

_____

_____

_____

_____

Ecclesiastes teaches us that our work and our projects are generally all worthwhile, but if we look to them as sources of ultimate meaning, we will invariably be disappointed. Remember what we have already noted: Eternity is the northward compass point of our hearts (Ecclesiastes 3:11). That means we can never be satisfied with temporal-based work.

How accurate is your inner spiritual compass? When you get turned around in this life, how quickly can you find "true north" again?

_____

_____

_____

_____

Old Testament commentator Derek Kidner makes this observation: "What spoils the pleasures of life for us is our hunger to get out of them more than they can ever deliver. Getting eternal and ultimate meaning out of temporal and temporary pursuits is destined to fail."

Reflect on what you're getting out of your temporal pursuits. Are you satisfied or dissatisfied? Why?

_____

_____

_____

_____

CHECKING YOUR PROGRESS
Think about your life in terms of Solomon's pursuits: wisdom, wild living, work, and wealth. Which one(s) reflect more of a temporal, rather than eternal, mind-set?

_____

_____

_____

_____

ASKING FOR DIRECTIONS
Write out a prayer that reflects your heart's desire about that area of your life. Ask that your heart might take on the values of heaven instead of earth:

_____

_____

_____

_____

Day 4

CAREENING CAREERS

DAILY READING: Ecclesiastes 2:11–26

KEY VERSE

For there is a man whose labor is with wisdom, knowledge, and skill; yet he must leave his heritage to a man who has not labored for it. This also is vanity and a great evil.
—Ecclesiastes 2:21

BIG IDEA

Accumulating mountains of money becomes meaningless to us within two seconds of death. In fact, the very reality of death strips our possessions of lasting significance. —DAVID JEREMIAH

EXCURSION JOURNAL

U. S. News and World Report recently [said]: "Today, work dominates Americans' lives as never before, as workers pile on hours at a rate not seen since the Industrial Revolution. Many workers are left feeling insecure, unfulfilled, and under-appreciated. . . . It's no wonder surveys of today's workers show a steady decline in job satisfaction. . . . People are feeling crushed."

Reflect on the role work plays in your life—and how you feel about it:

_____
_____
_____
_____
_____

Our culture is a cotton candy world—sugary, seductive, a pink swirl of empty calories. Today you might be the "flavor of the month," with Hollywood or Wall Street at your command. Tomorrow your pockets may be as empty as your soul.

12

Recall your own experience with the empty calories of this world's attractions:

_____
_____
_____
_____
_____

The wisdom, the work, and the pleasure of a good meal are no more than the appetizers, but they are good appetizers. We can enjoy our good homes and families; the pleasure of our recreation; the chilled swim and the grilled steak. We can feel good in connecting with our work. These things will never give us the one great pleasure that lies at the center of life, but they will complement it. They will cluster around the great shining star of godly contentment like lesser lights that point to the greatness of what is at the center.

Explain how you find the balance between enjoying God's good gifts without making them "the great shining star" of your life:

_____
_____
_____
_____
_____

We can smile as we watch Solomon dismantle the idea that God is in His heaven peering through the clouds to catch people having fun, so that He might put a stop to it. The God of Ecclesiastes is nothing like that; He is the Joygiver, the dispenser of pleasurable pursuits. Christ, the Bread of Life, leaves a little trail of good things like bread crumbs in the forest, leading straight to that joy that is heaven on earth: intimate fellowship with Him. Only in the aftertaste of that fellowship do these lesser tastes become truly pleasurable to us.

Be honest; to what degree do you see God as a joy-giver or joy-stealer, One who wants to catch you doing wrong instead of right?

_____
_____
_____
_____
_____

With open hearts and open hands, however, we understand that God lacks no resources and neither will we. The more of Him we discover and enjoy, the more we find available. Our hands joyfully open wider, and He gives from His infinitely generous heart. It is not the gifts that bring the joy, but He Himself; the gifts are simply His creative expression in telling us how much he loves us.

Reflect on the gifts you've received that most clearly speak to you of God's love:

_____

_____

_____

_____

_____

Would you rather be the first in line for wisdom and knowledge and joy, or would you rather be handed the heavy tools of "gathering and collecting" in service of the knowledge- and joy-getters? It's entirely your choice. If you decide to serve God, those wonderful gifts of wisdom and knowledge come with the deal. Otherwise, life is an unending round of heavy lifting.

How heavy do your hands feel at this point in your life? What tools are you wielding as you make your way in this world?

_____

_____

_____

_____

_____

CHECKING YOUR PROGRESS
Describe the level of contentment you live with regarding wealth and material goods. To what degree do you see them as potential or actual sources of pleasure?

_____

_____

_____

_____

_____

ASKING FOR DIRECTIONS

Write out Psalm 16:11 in your own words as a prayer for yourself concerning the true Source of temporal and eternal pleasure:

_____

_____

_____

_____

Day 5

IMPRESSIONS ABOUT LIFE

DAILY READING: Ecclesiastes 3:1–8

KEY VERSE
To everything there is a season, a time for every purpose under heaven. —
Ecclesiastes 3:1

BIG IDEA
Through all the seasons and circumstances of life, our lives need to reflect God's divine pacing—the cadence of His call and the rhythm of His wisdom.

—DAVID JEREMIAH

EXCURSION JOURNAL
Knowing there must be pain and suffering for us all, I dearly wish everyone could travel the road I did. I wish every human soul could see the face of God in the fear and turmoil. So many walk a very different path; they experience only His absence.

Recall a time in your life when suffering brought you closer to "the face of God":

_____

_____

_____

_____

_____

_____

_____

_____

In chapter 3 of Ecclesiastes, [Solomon] concludes that God is sovereign and in control, regardless of the imponderables that remain. . . . The king wants to know why God doesn't improve the standard of life, do something about the aging process, show more favoritism to His children, and perhaps discontinue the program of human pain.

Describe a circumstance that caused you to wonder the same things Solomon wondered, and how you resolved your questions:

_____

_____

_____

_____

We build up in our early years, and we start breaking down as we get older—painful but true. Someone said we know we're getting older when the type gets smaller, the steps get higher, the voices get softer, the muscles get weaker, and our medicine chest gets larger.

What evidence is there in your life of the reliability of the aging process? How are you responding to it?

_____

_____

_____

_____

_____

_____

Your tears are God's jewels; they are precious to Him. The greater your suffering, the greater His ministry and grace for you. We need to laugh, but sometimes we must also cry. The Lord is near us in both sadness and gladness. One day, He'll wipe away every tear from our eyes and the days of crying will be forgotten. But for now, there's a time to laugh and a time to weep.

Recall times in your life when God was present in both sadness and gladness:

_____

_____

_____

_____

_____

The more we talk, the more likely we are to sin (Proverbs 10:19); the fire of gossip dies out as soon as the talk ceases (26:20). In short, words can contain life or death—it is up to us to choose them carefully (18:21). There is no greater wisdom than knowing the seasons of the tongue—when it is time to speak and when it is time to keep silent (26:4–5).

Describe the greatest lesson you ever learned about the power of the tongue:

_____

_____

_____

_____

What Solomon is teaching us in Ecclesiastes 3:1–8 is that all of life unfolds under the appointment of providence: birth and death, sowing and harvest, joys and sorrows, acquiring and losing, speech and silence, war and peace—everything has its appointed time from God. He is sovereign, but He is always faithful.

How would you describe the time God has appointed for your life at present? What do you believe is His purpose?

_____

_____

_____

_____

_____

CHECKING YOUR PROGRESS

What is the biggest obstacle to your believing that there is "a time for every purpose under heaven"?

_____

_____

_____

_____

_____

_____

ASKING FOR DIRECTIONS

Write out a prayer that focuses on that obstacle. Ask God for faith to believe that everything in your life has its time and purpose in His plan.

_____

_____

_____

_____

_____

_____

Day 6

Insights About God

Daily Reading: Ecclesiastes 3:9–11

Key Verse

He has made everything beautiful in its time. Also He has put eternity in their hearts, except that no one can find out the work that God does from beginning to end.
—Ecclesiastes 3:11

Big Idea

When you stand back and view the great cavalcade of human experience from the divine perspective, God's fingerprints cover everything—the places of misery and tragedy most of all.

—David Jeremiah

Excursion Journal

In verse 10, Solomon says our busywork can obscure the true meaning of life unless we stop and take a close look. In so doing, we realize that God's plan is good. The truth is, "He has made everything beautiful in its time."

Recall something in your life that you know, without a doubt, God made "beautiful in its time":

_____

_____

_____

_____

_____

_____

_____

Life is not empty and random and godless, but full and precisely aligned and God-ordained. It's not that your most important work is meaningless; it's that your most trivial movements are also significant.

Describe a part of your life that seems trivial—something you have a hard time seeing God's hand in. Why is it hard to see Him?

_____

_____

_____

_____

_____

What profit has the worker? Much profit, if our tasks are God-given and Christ-centered. The real question is, "Am I doing what God wants me to do? Am I in the place, above all others, that He wants me to occupy?"

Write down your perspective on the place you are in now. Include the reasons you have for thinking it is, or isn't, the place He wants you to occupy right now.

_____

_____

_____

_____

_____

The game of Monopoly offers a "Get out of jail free" card, but God offers no such card to Christians. We must take the rain with the sun, the dark with the light, and know that God is painting a beautiful picture which requires all the tones, all the colors, all the depths of suffering as well as joy.

Describe the tones, colors, and depths that God has used to paint a recent experience in your life that was difficult.

_____

_____

_____

_____

_____

Malcolm Muggeridge . . . wrote the following in his book *A Twentieth Century Testimony:* "If it ever were to be possible to eliminate affliction from our earthly existence by means of some drug or other medical mumbo jumbo, as Aldous Huxley envisaged in *Brave New World*, the result would not be to make life delectable, but to make it too banal and trivial to be endurable."

Respond to Muggeridge's thesis. Would you prefer to live in an affliction-free world? Why or why not?

The choice is this: to be beat up, or to be upbeat. To say with Jacob in Genesis 42:36: *All these things are against me.* Or to say with Paul in Romans 8:28: *All things work together for good to those who love God. . . .* The perspective you choose will color your life completely and thoroughly—will it be gentle tones of grace and providence, or harsh slashes of despair and emptiness?

Paint a verbal picture of the perspective you choose most often in your life when difficulties arise:

If you don't learn to trust God, you will do one of two things: You will invent a god who has no basis in fact, as my friend the rabbi did. Or you will believe in the true God but live in a constant state of agitation because He doesn't act the way you think He should or explain to you what you think you deserve to know. We must trust God to be God.

In what kind of circumstances are you most tempted to play God?

God has put something in our hearts—a taste or longing for eternity—that cannot be discovered through the experiences of life. There will always be a longing within us for something more than we have experienced until we know God personally.

Describe the first sense you had that there was something eternal missing from your experience:

_____

_____

_____

_____

_____

Catherine Marshall . . . wrote about her anguish over the death of a beloved grandchild. . . . : "When life hands us situations we cannot understand, we have one of two choices: We can wallow in misery, separated from God. Or we can tell Him, "I need You and Your presence in my life more than I need understanding. I choose You, Lord. I trust You to give me understanding and an answer to all of my whys, only if and when You choose."

If you are facing a situation you cannot understand, describe the choice you have made and how you are manifesting it in your life:

_____

_____

_____

_____

CHECKING YOUR PROGRESS
In what places(s) have you found God's fingerprints lately—a place you were surprised to find evidence of a good and loving God. Why were you surprised?

_____

_____

_____

_____

_____

ASKING FOR DIRECTIONS
Use Psalm 119:71 as inspiration for a prayer in which you confess your willingness to discover evidence of God's hand in even your darkest hour. ("It is good for me that I have been afflicted, that I may learn Your statutes.")

_____

_____

_____

_____

_____

_____

_____

_____

Day 7

READ THE INSTRUCTIONS

DAILY READING: Ecclesiastes 3:12–15

KEY VERSE
I know that whatever God does, it shall be forever. Nothing can be added to it, and nothing taken from it. God does it, that men should fear before Him.—Ecclesiastes 3:14

BIG IDEA
The Westminster Catechism has it right: "Man's chief and highest end is to glorify God, and to enjoy Him forever."

—DAVID JEREMIAH

EXCURSION JOURNAL
Life—the awesome gift of God—shouldn't be afflicted by the paralysis of analysis. We'll either be frozen in fear over what comes next, or we'll become so confused over the meaning of it all that we won't notice the joy leaking out through the seams of everyday living.

How introspective are you? How much second-guessing do you do? How do you find a healthy balance between questioning and faith?

_____

_____

_____

_____

_____

God cannot be put into any convenient box of our design. As Archie Bunker once said (with painfully mangled theology), "That's how He got to be God." Besides, poking too far into the matter is how we got to be in *our* present state.

Reflect on your willingness to let God be God when you lack answers in life:

_____

_____

_____

_____

I think when most Christians approach the end of life, they're going to wish they had served God more faithfully. But I think they'll have another regret—that they didn't fully take advantage of the wonderful abundance in life that Christ offers us.

How do you respond to these two potential end-of-life reflections?

_____

_____

_____

_____

_____

_____

God enjoys our enjoyment! He fills the world with good things for a reason. Go to a football game. Spend time with your family. Take a vacation. Pursue an enjoyable hobby. Relax in the sauna. Do a little something for yourself every day and thank God for the blessings He has abundantly poured into your life.

How free are you to do things for yourself purely for the pleasure of it? What is the basis of your freedom (or lack of it)?

_____

_____

_____

_____

_____

_____

In a memorial service . . . "What I'm Thankful For" . . . [Helen Sunday] began like this: "Folks, it's surprising how many things God can reveal to you to be thankful for, if you really want to know and ask Him to help you. I had no idea there were so many!"

Remind yourself of the things you are most thankful for in your life:

_____

_____

_____

_____

_____

_____

Optimistic people see blessings amidst burdens. They realize the sun always breaks through sooner or later. It refuses to be defined by the presence of dark clouds. After all, the dark clouds are nothing but mist; the sun is built to last.

To what degree do you tend to see the proverbial glass half empty or half full? Why do you see life as you do?

_____

_____

_____

_____

_____

Life? We have no reason to fear it. God? We have every reason. We fear His magnificence, His infinity, His wrath, and therefore we fear the prospect of ever wandering from His friendship, ever turning from His presence, ever losing His power, as Solomon did.

Record the actions or practices in your life which manifest a healthy fear (respect, honor) of God:

_____

_____

_____

_____

_____

_____

CHECKING YOUR PROGRESS
We know it's a sin not to fear God. Comment on why not enjoying God might be just as significant a failure:

_____

_____

_____

_____

_____

_____

_____

_____

_____

_____

ASKING FOR DIRECTIONS

Compose a prayer of praise and thanks to God, expressing your reverence for who He is and your thanks for all His good gifts:

_____

_____

_____

_____

_____

_____

_____

_____

_____

_____

_____

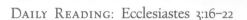

Day 8

WHEN JUSTICE ISN'T JUST

DAILY READING: Ecclesiastes 3:16–22

KEY VERSE
I said in my heart, "God shall judge the righteous and the wicked, for there is a time there for every purpose and for every work." —Ecclesiastes 3:17

BIG IDEA
Justice is coming, whether today, tomorrow, or in a thousand lifetimes; it is as certain as death, the fate of the just and the unjust. And living in bitterness is not worth the trouble, while joy is worth any price.

—DAVID JEREMIAH

EXCURSION JOURNAL
If there is a God of love, justice, and power, how do you explain the fact that life isn't fair, and cruel injustices may stand? It's a story as old as humanity. The guilty walk free while the innocent suffer.

What is your response to the question above?

_____
_____
_____
_____
_____
_____
_____
_____

This deeply bothered Solomon—injustice under the sun. The wicked prosper in their sins while the righteous suffer in their integrity. People with money can oil the wheels of justice, making them turn in their direction and in their favor, while the poor often find themselves at the mercy of an overburdened court nearly bursting at the seams.

Recall a time when you were tempted to "grease the wheels" of some system to your advantage. What thoughts went through your mind? What did you do?

_____

_____

_____

_____

_____

Solomon uses a unique literary technique to make his point. With characteristic honesty, he tells it exactly as he sees it, using the phrase "I saw" no less than four times in this section (Ecclesiastes 3:16; 4:4, 7, 15). He takes a look around, records his observations, and draws his own conclusions.

Have you seen injustices you could have addressed but didn't? What held you back?

_____

_____

_____

_____

_____

"While I was there," Soon Ok Lee, speaking of North Korea, said, "I never saw Christians deny their faith. Not one. When these Christians were silent, the officers would become furious and kick them. At the time, I could not understand why they risked their lives when they could have said, 'I do not believe,' and done what the officers wanted. I even saw many who sang hymns as the kicking and hitting intensified. The officers would call them crazy and take them to the electric-treatment room. I didn't see one come out alive."

How do you think you would respond in a brutally unfair situation—especially one where denying your faith would release you from suffering?

_____

_____

_____

_____

_____

We hate it when someone "gets away with it."

Recall a time when someone close to you profited unjustly—and didn't acknowledge it. What should you do in such a situation?

_____

_____

_____

_____

_____

_____

Small and all—good ways to characterize the extent of God's present and future judgment. As someone said, "In the choir of life, it's easy to fake the words—but someday each of us will have to sing solo before God."

How much does a future evaluation before God influence your daily life? How much should it?

_____

_____

_____

_____

_____

_____

Let's get personal here. Have you ever been the victim of injustice? Perhaps you received a speeding ticket when, in fact, you were well within the speed zone. Perhaps a coworker slandered you, preventing you from getting the promotion you deserved. Maybe an associate or family member accused you falsely. What should you do about it?

Recall a time when you were treated unjustly, what you did about it, and what you learned from it:

_____

_____

_____

_____

_____

_____

There is wisdom and comfort in realizing that because life goes on, we can go on with life. Yes, injustices will go on as well on this side of eternity. Life isn't fair—never was, never will be.

Describe a situation that you have purposed will not keep you from going on with life:

_____
_____
_____
_____
_____
_____

CHECKING YOUR PROGRESS
Think about how long it takes you to recover when judged unjustly in this world. What would you like to see changed about your response in terms of time and temperament?

_____
_____
_____
_____
_____
_____
_____
_____
_____

ASKING FOR DIRECTIONS
In light of Genesis 18:25—"Shall not the Judge of all the earth do right?"—write out a prayer asking God for grace to trust Him when you are judged unjustly:

_____
_____
_____
_____
_____
_____

Day 9

FROM OPPRESSION TO OBSESSION

DAILY READING: Ecclesiastes 4:1–6

KEY VERSE
Better a handful with quietness than both hands full, together with toil and grasping for the wind.—Ecclesiastes 4:6

BIG IDEA
Help us indeed to be content, Lord, in the pleasant valley between too much and too little; between slavery and sloth; between overcompeting and underperforming.
—DAVID JEREMIAH

EXCURSION JOURNAL
Most of us have endured midnights of the soul. In such moments we can thank God that we know He has a better place for us; we need only be patient. But what about those with no belief in heaven? What can we say to the temporally oppressed and eternally hopeless?

Reflect on how you handled "midnights of the soul" before you became a Christian? How do you handle them differently now?

_____

_____

_____

_____

_____

_____

_____

Through my years in ministry I've come to the conclusion that sometimes it's best to simply say, "I don't know. I wish I could give you a full and satisfying answer to your question." We would be foolish to claim an understanding of all the intricacies of God's ways, when in truth we comprehend so little of them.

Describe your personal comfort level with saying "I don't know" when you are in turmoil or pain. Should God provide you with all the answers?

_____

_____

_____

_____

_____

_____

We look at our jobs, our governments, and everything else through our own hazy viewpoints. Then, perhaps in church, perhaps in prayer, perhaps on some other holy ground, we gaze through the portal of "the sanctuary of God." The picture changes, like a kaleidoscope of dark colors shifting into a beautiful moonlight landscape. The colors all remain, but we begin to get the picture, too. God's perspective is based on different parameters—His love, His grace, His eternal purposes—and the moment we begin to account for these, we make wiser judgments about what we see under the sun.

What kind of "sanctuary setting" helps keep your focus on God sharp when life begins to get blurry around the edges?

_____

_____

_____

_____

_____

_____

Solomon's message for you and me is, "As we look upon the oppressed, our hearts are broken. We'd rather not see; we'd rather fix our minds on pleasant subjects. But how can we turn our backs on God's beloved children? We must look hard and accept that we don't have all the answers. Our Lord does, and we'll understand it better by and by."

How do you know "by and by" is not just "pie in the sky"? What gives you confidence that you really will understand injustices like the fate of the oppressed?

_____

_____

_____

_____

The headline read, "Professional Jealousy Grips the Nation": "Almost nine out of ten office workers suffer from "professional envy" of colleagues they perceive to have more glamorous or better paid jobs, according to a survey by Office Angels. The survey of 1,500 office workers by the recruitment consultancy found more than two-thirds of respondents felt professional jealousy toward friends who made their own working life appear bland in comparison. Almost a third envy a partner or spouse's job, while a fifth feel jealous of a work colleague who is further up the career ladder."

In what area of life does envy, jealousy, or covetousness tempt you the most? How do you handle such temptations?

_____
_____
_____
_____
_____
_____

Neither overcompeting nor underperforming is the answer. Solomon suggests the true solution in 4:6: "Better a handful with quietness than both hands full, together with toil and grasping for the wind." Translation: *Seek balance.* One hand filled with prosperity, contentment, and quietness, is far better than two hands filled with envy and rivalry.

Reflect on a time or setting in which you found Solomon's teaching to be true:

_____
_____
_____
_____
_____
_____
_____
_____
_____

Every one of us involved in a race to accumulate the most toys will come out the loser in the end.

Describe your standing in the race to accumulate the most toys in this life:

_____

_____

_____

_____

_____

_____

CHECKING YOUR PROGRESS
What is the greatest area of discontent in your life? Can you identify its source?

_____

_____

_____

_____

_____

_____

_____

_____

_____

_____

ASKING FOR DIRECTIONS
Meditate on 1 Timothy 6:8 ("And having food and clothing, with these we shall be content") and compose a prayer of contentment to God in which you thank Him for what you do and don't have.

_____

_____

_____

_____

_____

_____

_____

_____

_____

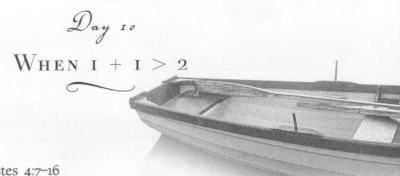

Day 10

WHEN 1 + 1 > 2

DAILY READING: Ecclesiastes 4:7-16

KEY VERSE
Though one may be overpowered by another, two can withstand him. And a threefold cord is not quickly broken.—Ecclesiastes 4:12

BIG IDEA
The crowns and congratulations of the world cannot compare to the crowns that will one day come from the nail-scarred hands of Jesus Christ.
—DAVID JEREMIAH

EXCURSION JOURNAL
But consider a relationship wound—and we're not even considering divorces, lawsuits, or the truly serious issues. Just think about the last time someone you care about said something that really hurt. Someone hit a nerve of the emotional variety, and I would predict that in one year, two years, maybe even a decade, you'll remember exactly what was said and how you felt. Only time and God heal wounds like that.

Reflect on an emotional hurt that you have not forgotten. Does not forgetting mean not forgiving? Why or why not?

_____

_____

_____

_____

_____

_____

We know that life's most perilous task may well be that of maintaining an emotionally and spiritually successful family.

What has your experience with family taught you about the perilous nature of being part of one?

_____

_____

_____

_____

_____

But there is a cost as well as a payout to our work. We all begin with the same number of minutes, and we invest them however we choose. If the bulk of our investment is in work, our relationship portfolio will be very weak.

What has been your experience, positive and negative, with keeping work balanced with relationships?

_____

_____

_____

_____

_____

We see images of the unforgettable character of Ebenezer Scrooge, created by Charles Dickens, sitting up by himself on Christmas Eve, eating his soup before a fire small enough for one. All the rich furnishings around him are slowly going to dust and mold, for who is there to share them with? Why polish the windows when no one looks in or out? He was a rich man, but money bought him no friends; in fact, it seemed to do the very opposite. Do the math and you'll discover that $1 + 0 = 0$.

Explain the formula $1 + 0 = 0$. Is this formula accurate based on your experience?

_____

_____

_____

_____

_____

Two human souls combine their strength, creativity, talent, and ambition. Synergy (the intangible chemistry of working together) takes over. You share the work but you also share a greater reward. The whole can be greater than the sum of its parts. When you do the math, you find that $1 + 1$ adds up to some value greater than two.

Explain a way in which "relationships synergy" has benefited you:

_____
_____
_____
_____
_____

I pity the person who has no friends to lean on when life gets hard. Not only does he face the difficulties of life, but he faces the discouragement and loneliness of confronting those challenges alone.

Do you have enough people to lean on when life gets hard? What have you done lately to increase that number? For whom could you become a person to lean on?

_____
_____
_____
_____
_____

In truth, Solomon shouldn't even have to remind us of such obvious facts of life. But there are many who try to go it alone as much as possible, and it is for these true lone rangers that Solomon makes his point. "Woe to him who is alone when he falls."

From your experience, describe what it feels like to fall alone. Why isn't God all we need in those times?

_____
_____
_____
_____
_____

We can be attacked physically, but also spiritually, emotionally, or financially. The world is filled with snares, and there is wonderful security in the feeling of community we have. It's heartbreaking to read of people who grow old without the comfort of friends and family.

Reflect on the ways in which you are glad that "two are better than one" in your life:

_____
_____
_____

_____

_____

Are you struggling to make and keep friends? Are some of your relationships going sour? Don't worry so much about *making* friends; work at *being* a friend. Solomon writes elsewhere: "A man who has friends must himself be friendly" (Proverbs 18:24). Dale Carnegie observed that we can make more friends in two months of showing interest in others, than in two years of trying to get them interested in us.

Can you validate Solomon's and Dale Carnegie's words from your experience? Recall different seasons of your life when you were, and weren't, a good friend—and the results:

_____

_____

_____

_____

_____

Fame is like a lover to avoid: beautiful to the eye, seductive to the spirit, and fickle to the end. Fame is expensive, requiring obsessive pursuit. Once apprehended, its attractions are not only fleeting but profoundly disappointing.

CHECKING YOUR PROGRESS
Describe the degree to which you are bound together in a strong cord with others. How has that strength been an asset or a liability?

_____

_____

_____

_____

_____

ASKING FOR DIRECTIONS
Compose a prayer asking God to give you creativity in binding yourself strongly to others:

_____

_____

_____

_____

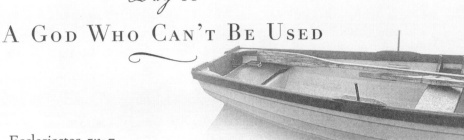

Day 11

A GOD WHO CAN'T BE USED

DAILY READING: Ecclesiastes 5:1–7

KEY VERSE

For in the multitude of dreams and many words there is also vanity. But fear God.
—Ecclesiastes 5:7

BIG IDEA

A promise to God, honored by the one who made it, can lead to a touch of heaven on earth. But a vow in danger of being broken is an idea that should make us shudder with fear.—DAVID JEREMIAH

EXCURSION JOURNAL

One woman, having lost both her husband and son in separate accidents, posted a notice on the Internet: "I am ANGRY at God. I am VERY ANGRY!" She dared to say out loud what you and I really feel sometimes.

What is the most emotionally charged thing you have ever said to God? Did you let it stand, or take it back?

_____
_____
_____
_____
_____

God understands our anger, and when we pray it's a good thing to tell Him what we honestly feel. But sustained bitterness toward the Lord who loves us is irrational and unwise.

Describe a time when you had a hard time forgiving God. What did you learn about your role and His role?

_____
_____
_____
_____

Imagine stumbling into the house of God loaded down with a heavy burden. It's the dead weight of all your sorrows. You're certainly bringing them to the right place, but you need to bring them in the right way. When you're overloaded, it's important to watch your step.

If you have ever missed your step and fallen because of the burden you were carrying, describe how you managed to get back on your feet before God:

Life without boundaries is chaos, and when we treat God as if He is not in control and not loving, when we cut Him down to our size through a petty approach, when we wander outside of the boundaries between us, we invite chaos into our lives.

What have you learned along the way—from parents, teachers, from God—about the necessity for respecting boundaries? for practicing self-control?

Could [God] start a fire? *Of course.* Could He also prevent or suppress one? *Yes.* Could it be that He has, so many times in many places all the time, without any human being realizing it? *Yes!* That's something we seldom consider. We see every fire God allows but none that He prevents.

Recall an experience of escaping something bad that you didn't find out about until much later. Did you give God credit for the save?

Solomon would feel differently. He reminds us that God knows the time and appointed season of every life. He counts the very hairs on your head, and a sparrow doesn't plummet to earth without His awareness. And as Jesus tells us, "You are of more value than many sparrows" (Matthew 10:31).

Has there been a time when you felt you weren't more valuable "than many sparrows" to God? What has convinced you that you are?

_____

_____

_____

_____

_____

_____

Solomon counsels us to be men and women of few words, for the mark of a fool is his airy gust of reckless speech.

When did you most recently release the "airy gust of reckless speech" before God or others? What is the solution to this ever-present temptation?

_____

_____

_____

_____

_____

_____

There are times when God uses a storm or crisis to awaken us, and we make life-changing vows and commitments to Him. The problem is that most of us are quicker to make a commitment than we are to keep it. We live in an age of halfhearted vows and ill-kept promises.

Describe what you have learned from experience about the dangers of making, but not keeping, commitments to God and others:

_____

_____

_____

_____

_____

CHECKING YOUR PROGRESS
Why do unfulfilled vows (promises, commitments) defile the conscience? Identify any commitment, be it small or large, that you have made but not kept:

_____
_____
_____
_____
_____
_____
_____
_____
_____
_____

ASKING FOR DIRECTIONS
Compose a prayer to God asking for strength and honor to fulfill vows you have made or will make, or for forgiveness for any you made which cannot now be fulfilled:

_____
_____
_____
_____
_____
_____
_____
_____
_____
_____

Day 12

GOVERNMENTS NEVER CHANGE

DAILY READING: Ecclesiastes 5:8–9

KEY VERSE
Moreover the profit of the land is for all; even the king is served from the field.
—Ecclesiastes 5:9

BIG IDEA
Heaven on earth cannot be established at the ballot box but only through the hearts of men. And on that day we will see the descent of the New Jerusalem, we will know that there is, at last, one Governor before whom to bow, with no more use for intermediaries; one Party to serve, with no more use for debate or dissension; one Lord, one faith, one baptism into the world that has always been our destiny as His divine constituency.—DAVID JEREMIAH

EXCURSION JOURNAL
We expect the system to fail occasionally, and we have to wash out the stains every now and then, keeping the laundry of state as pure and clean as possible. Therefore, we cheer on the honest representatives and leaders and use the system to uproot those who break the trust. But we cherish no illusions of keeping the machine in perfect repair. This is Solomon's point: Creeping corruption cannot be prevented.

Paint a verbal picture of your overall attitude toward civil government as evidenced by your involvement, prayers, and level of respect:

_____
_____
_____
_____

The failings of governments are nothing more than the failings of men. . . . Anyone who puts his hope in the government is surely bound to be disappointed. That doesn't mean we don't appreciate the righteous things government does. It just means that our ultimate hope for protection and salvation is in a God who never disappoints.

Reflect on how often you find yourself disappointed with government, expressing your disappointment to others. What does that suggest about the ultimate object of your trust?

_____

_____

_____

_____

In that regard, looking at the government is like looking in a mirror. If you feel the government should be doing a much better job of governing the people, what about the job you are doing governing your life? Are there integrity issues? Health issues? Effective use of time and resources?

Record your own answers to the above questions:

_____

_____

_____

_____

_____

Every ruler in this world serves at God's pleasure—and so do you in your own position, for that matter. Our God is in control of everything; why should we think His divine authority ends on the Capitol steps?

How do you reconcile the above statement with the unjust and inhumane actions of world leaders?

_____

_____

_____

_____

We are to pray for our officials. Paul commands, "Therefore I exhort first of all that supplications, prayers, intercessions, and giving of thanks be made for all men, for kings and all who are in authority, that we may lead a quiet and peaceable life in all godliness and reverence" (1 Timothy 2:1–2). How often do you actually pray for your president, your elected representatives, your governors, mayors, and council members?

Answer the above question, then reflect on your attitude toward government in light of your answer:

_____
_____
_____
_____

We obey our leaders loyally, knowing that in serving them, we serve God. An ordinance is a law. Many of us have grown cynical about our laws and duties toward them. Be an upholder of the law and a proactive servant of the public good in your community.

Reflect on your attitude toward the smallest laws of the land—speed limits, littering, traffic ordinances—in light of James 2:10: "For whoever shall keep the whole law, and yet stumble in one point, he is guilty of all."

_____
_____
_____
_____
_____

And we realize that Christians must walk the tightrope of respecting government . . . while working within it to the glory of God.

How would you express to a new Christian the responsibility to respect government while working to change it at the same time?

_____
_____
_____
_____
_____

CHECKING YOUR PROGRESS
Contrast your attitude toward and involvement in our nation's systems of governance since you came to know Christ:

_____
_____
_____
_____
_____

ASKING FOR DIRECTIONS

Write a prayer for our nation's leaders expressing what you would like to see God do in their lives for the benefit of the governed and for His glory:

_____

_____

_____

_____

_____

_____

Day 13

DOLLARS AND SENSE

DAILY READING: Ecclesiastes 5:10–20

KEY VERSE
As for every man to whom God has given riches and wealth, and given him power to eat of it, to receive his heritage and rejoice in his labor—this is the gift of God.—Ecclesiastes 5:19

BIG IDEA
Every good and perfect gift comes from God and has a good and perfect use. As long as we can find it and honor it, we honor him.—DAVID JEREMIAH

EXCURSION JOURNAL
In the realm of faith, we require a certain kind of nourishment. As the body thirsts for water and the lungs yearn for air, so the soul is hungry for heaven. We feed ourselves through His Word, His presence, His service, and His vision for us—so many good and healthy nutrients. He has set a full table before us, and we need only share the banquet.

How would you gauge your spiritual health? Describe your spiritual "feeding habits" and the nutrients you are consuming:

_____
_____
_____
_____
_____

We live on earth but our true home is heaven, and that creates a distance in the soul. We will never be at peace until we find the bridge between the two worlds. So we continue the search for the things that really matter in life—for heaven on earth.

To what degree would you say you are still searching for heaven on earth via material things?

_____

_____

_____

_____

And when life goes wrong, we look first to the financial remedy. Her marriage fails, and she wonders if a bigger house would have made the difference. He faces depression, so he goes out and buys an expensive sports car. They're losing their kids, so they shower them with gifts. *Very simply, wealth is not the answer.*

Describe a time when you have used wealth as the answer to a stressful situation. What did you learn?

_____

_____

_____

_____

_____

Wouldn't it be wonderful to be truly content? To be eased of the burden for more accumulation, and to be at peace with where we are in life? Why do we make ourselves miserable over what has no track record of satisfying?

How would you answer the last question above? Recall your own track record with using material things to satisfy:

_____

_____

_____

_____

_____

When the San Diego County fires began approaching our neighborhood, the order came to collect our valuables and evacuate our homes. Driving down the hill from our home, I turned to Donna and said, "Do you realize it only took us ten minutes to collect our valuables? Everything else is just 'stuff.'"

How long would it take you to collect your valuables in a similar situation? What would you take with you; what are your valuables?

_____

_____

_____

_____

_____

But motives tell the tale, and the American tale lacks a spiritual premise, for there is no such thing as a self-made man or woman. Every person who ever earned a dime did so with a heart, mind, soul, strength, talents, and opportunities supplied by God.

How does your pride respond to the idea that there is no such thing as a self-made man or woman?

_____

_____

_____

_____

_____

God gives us not only the gift, but the ability to enjoy it: the food and the mouth to eat it; the art and the mind to appreciate it; the beautiful earth and the feet to run upon it. Every component of life, down to the smallest molecule, is part of His gift. But we cannot enjoy any gift properly without reference to the Giver.

How does knowing that something (everything) has its source in God change your stewardship of it?

_____

_____

_____

_____

_____

Every good and perfect gift comes from God and has a good and perfect use. As long as we can find it and honor it, we honor Him. And we are one step closer to heaven on earth, rather than one foot deeper into the golden mirage of a fool's paradise.

Have you ever unleashed "hell on earth" by your misuse of a gift of God? What did you learn from the experience?

_____

_____

_____

_____

_____

CHECKING YOUR PROGRESS

Are there any of God's gifts you are unsure how to use for His glory? (Reflect on what it means to use a camping trailer or a boat or a second home for God's glory.)

_____

_____

_____

_____

_____

_____

_____

_____

_____

ASKING FOR DIRECTIONS

Using David's prayer in 1 Chronicles 29:14 as a model ("For all things come from You, and of Your own we have given You"), compose your own confessional prayer to God, thanking Him for all His good gifts—especially any that you may not have thought to thank Him for before:

_____

_____

_____

_____

_____

_____

_____

_____

_____

Day 14

MONEY WITHOUT MEANING

DAILY READING: Ecclesiastes 6:1–6

KEY VERSE
A man to whom God has given riches and wealth and honor, so that he lacks nothing for himself of all he desires; yet God does not give him power to eat of it, but a foreigner consumes it. This is vanity, and it is an evil affliction.—Ecclesiastes 6:2

BIG IDEA
Life without God and without meaning is worse than never having been born at all.—DAVID JEREMIAH

EXCURSION JOURNAL
One study claims that instant millionaires have about the same level of happiness as accident victims. . . . Yet people still line up at convenience stores and gas stations across the nation to put down their money for a chance at unhappiness.

What is your perspective on opportunities for instant wealth (lotteries, sweepstakes, etc.)? Do you see them as a potential source of happiness? Why or why not?

_____

_____

_____

_____

_____

Story after story can be cited of people whose newfound fame and fortune have made them more miserable than when they were just average citizens. Some people manage to keep heart and home together, but their stories are few and far between.

If you have known someone who was made instantly rich, what impact did it have on his or her life? How did his or her experience change your thinking?

_____

_____

_____

_____

_____

When [Solomon] was twenty, the Lord appeared to him as he worshiped and invited him to ask anything he desired. Solomon asked for wisdom, and God was pleased.

Truthfully, what would you ask God for if you were given the same invitation as Solomon?

_____

_____

_____

_____

_____

_____

He blesses us "exceedingly abundantly above all that we ask or think, according to the power that works in us" (Ephesians 3:20). Our cups overflow, and goodness and mercy follow us all the days of our lives.

Reflect on a way that God has blessed you far beyond what you could have asked or imagined:

_____

_____

_____

_____

_____

_____

Foreign women brought their idolatrous worship into Solomon's life. Tragically, the king's spiritual center, God Himself, gradually was moved more and more to the sideline of his life. "For it was so, when Solomon was old, that his wives turned his heart after other gods; and his heart was not loyal to the LORD his God" (1 Kings 11:4).

Have you ever allowed materialism to distract you from worshiping God? What did you learn in the process?

_____

_____

_____

_____

_____

_____

On the other hand, life *with* God is deeply satisfying, whether one has little or much. It's not the years in life, but the life in the years. Only God can give us the wisdom to know what to do with what we have.

Reflect on different seasons in your life; when you had little, and when you had more. Compare the two seasons in terms of spiritual growth, gratitude, and enjoyment:

_____

_____

_____

_____

_____

_____

We need not disappear into the golden quicksand of our wealth, as Solomon did, and as countless other souls have done. That quicksand is a valley of lost souls. It is among the most treacherous tests we face on the trail to find what counts in life.

Recall a time when the quicksand of wealth became a source of danger for you. How did you escape? Or are you still trapped?

_____

_____

_____

_____

_____

_____

_____

_____

CHECKING YOUR PROGRESS

Describe the degree to which you are making progress in your life with regard to the acquisition and use of wealth:

_____

_____

_____

_____

_____

ASKING FOR DIRECTIONS

Agur prayed that God would give him neither poverty nor riches for fear he would steal on the one hand or forget about God on the other (Proverbs 30:8–9). Compose your own prayer to God expressing the desire of your heart regarding material wealth:

_____

_____

_____

_____

_____

_____

_____

Day 15

EMPLOYMENT WITHOUT ENJOYMENT

DAILY READING: Ecclesiastes 6:7–9

KEY VERSE
Better is the sight of the eyes than the wandering of desire. This also is vanity and grasping for the wind.—Ecclesiastes 6:9

BIG IDEA
Work is a compelling, fruitful, gracious gift from God—but not the ultimate source of joy in this life.—DAVID JEREMIAH

EXCURSION JOURNAL
I find genuine joy in my job, and I hope you do, too—whether you're a governor or a garbage collector.

Recount for your own benefit how you feel about your job. Are there any ways in which you are expecting more from your job than it can give?

_____
_____
_____
_____
_____

Work makes life compelling. It teaches us about ourselves. It gives us the pleasure of fruitfulness. But if you approach your job as the reason for being here, you'll come to one more dead end.

What is it reasonable for you to expect and receive from the particular job you have? (Think of financial, emotional, relational, intellectual, and spiritual dimensions of life.)

_____
_____
_____
_____
_____

Jobs are earthly, and joy is heavenly. A job is not what really matters in life, but it offers a number of clues to what does. It's not the whole picture, but one more jigsaw puzzle piece that fits into the vast panorama we are developing of heaven on earth.

How big a piece of your life's puzzle does your job represent? Does all your (and your family's) life revolve around it?

We can and should work hard, and all of us do at times. But don't miss the caution flag Solomon is waving here: Trade those minutes and hours of your life carefully, for they repay you in the coin of the realm, which does not satisfy the hunger of the soul.

Is it possible to reap eternal benefits from your job as well as earthly benefits? How would that happen? Does your job provide some, or any, of both?

A wise man with the greatest education in the world has no ultimate advantage over a fool when God is absent from his life.

Recall a setting in which you were amazed at a person's intellectual abilities and his lack of spiritual depth. What does that tell you about the relationship of spiritual truth to intellectual capacity?

There is nothing wrong with dreaming and vision-casting. But if we live in a fantasy world, we live in a world that will likely never come to pass.

Are you moving forward or just treading water at this point in your life? If the latter, what would you need to do to start moving forward?

_____

_____

_____

_____

_____

_____

If your career is the determining factor in your life—you're constantly waiting for the next raise, the next promotion, the next assignment, the next transfer—then you are living with the "wandering of desire."

How do you avoid the "wandering of desire" while at the same time creating healthy dreams for the future?

_____

_____

_____

_____

_____

_____

What happens if you take a "surprise day off" for your family? You'll be one more day behind on the job, but think of the memories you'll make with your wife, kids, grandkids. Twenty years from now, which will matter more? One touches godly relationships with heavenly companions; the other is simply another acre plowed, another clock punched, another day, another dollar.

When was the last time you took a day off simply to do something you love? How did your conscience react to your decision?

_____

_____

_____

_____

_____

CHECKING YOUR PROGRESS
Describe your dream job—what you would do for a living if you had the opportunity:

_____
_____
_____
_____
_____
_____
_____
_____
_____

ASKING FOR DIRECTIONS
Compose a prayer thanking God for the work you have at present and asking Him to help you achieve the vocational desire of your heart:

_____
_____
_____
_____
_____
_____
_____
_____

Day 16

SOLOMON ANSWERS YOUR QUESTIONS

DAILY READING: Ecclesiastes 6:10–12

KEY VERSE
For who knows what is good for man in life, all the days of his vain life which he passes like a shadow? Who can tell a man what will happen after him under the sun?—Ecclesiastes 6:12

BIG IDEA
In Ecclesiastes, Solomon offers one core argument reflected in many different colors: Your life without God is meaningless.—DAVID JEREMIAH

EXCURSION JOURNAL
Readers will come to these pages from many different points on the spiritual compass. Some of you have grown wise in the seasons of life. . . . Others come from a direction of ongoing struggle. . . . Or perhaps you're just one of those many who are found somewhere in between.

From where in life did you come to the pages of The Search for Heaven on Earth? *What key adjectives would you use to describe your life right now?*

_____

_____

_____

_____

Where do you fit? What particular life issues do you bring to this book? I believe that there are many key moments in life: whenever the sermon begins, whenever you read the first page of a book, whenever you find yourself in a thoughtful conversation about life with a trusted friend. I don't believe these moments are random and coincidental, but that in some important way they are divine appointments, potential crossroad moments.

Recall the key turning points in your life—those crossroad moments that, looking back, seem to have been divine appointments:

_____

_____

_____

_____

I firmly believe that your reading of this book, like many of your other experiences, represents a "message moment" for you. And what you come away with will depend upon what you're willing to take seriously about this moment.

Describe to yourself your reasons for reading this book—what you wanted to get out of it:

_____

_____

_____

_____

_____

But I hope you'll stop right here, too, and reflect a bit on what is happening in your life between God, His Word, this book, and your future. I would predict that if you are facing some of the serious issues about your life and your values, you will find yourself encountering some personal turmoil. You could be saying, "My approach to God needs to change," or "I've been making wealth the center of my life."

What has God been saying to your heart as you have read this book?

_____

_____

_____

_____

_____

He made us creatures who enjoy work, because He enjoys it. He made us creatures who enjoy gathering wealth, because He owns the cattle on one thousand hills. But He didn't make us to *exist* for these things—only to find and recognize Him more clearly through them.

What have you learned about God through the things you enjoy and do well?

_____

_____

_____

_____
_____
_____

Arguing with God is an exercise in futility.

Do you, or have you ever, argued with God? What about? What was the outcome? What was your response to the outcome?

_____
_____
_____
_____
_____

The right approach is to discover the plan of God and live it out; it is arrogance of a cosmic intensity to try and change the plan.

Is prayer an effort on your part to change "the plan"? Or does the plan incorporate your prayers? Why or why not?

_____
_____
_____
_____
_____
_____

We want [our children] to be happy, and when they stumble we often hurt more than they do. That's just the way God looks at us. We think we're pretty sharp and that we already have the answers. And God patiently keeps speaking to us through His Word, through His Spirit, through our believing friends, wishing we would trust Him just a little bit more than we do.

Do you ever roll your eyes and say, "Sure, God, whatever you say," the way a child might respond to his earthly father? How does God's patience with your responses give you patience with the responses of others?

_____
_____
_____
_____

The best way to be ready for the future is to stick close to God. He's the one in charge of it. Solomon says that trying to figure out the future for oneself is an exercise in vanity. . . . For that reason, arguing with Him will change nothing.

Why doesn't your trust in God turn into a form of fatalism? How do you keep your faith personal instead of abstract?

_____

_____

_____

_____

We don't know what the future holds, but we do know Who holds it—and that is enough. It ends every argument or objection we can pose. And coming to the end of all the questions, we can only bow before the One with all the answers.

Make some notes on questions you have for God that are unanswered. Also note the degree to which you are willing not to have them answered in this life:

_____

_____

_____

_____

_____

CHECKING YOUR PROGRESS
At the halfway point of the book, what is the single most meaningful thing you have gleaned from your reading? And what change(s) do you think might come from that insight?

_____

_____

_____

_____

ASKING FOR DIRECTIONS
Write out a prayer asking God for wisdom and purpose to make the change(s) you noted above:

_____

_____

_____

_____

_____

Day 17

THE JOY OF MISERY

DAILY READING: Ecclesiastes 7:1–4

KEY VERSE
The heart of the wise is in the house of mourning, but the heart of fools is in the house of mirth.—Ecclesiastes 7:4

BIG IDEA
The highest purpose of life is *not* happiness.—DAVID JEREMIAH

EXCURSION JOURNAL
It's not that Solomon is buying into the philosophy of despair. If that were true, he wouldn't tell us eight times in this book to enjoy life. I've underlined those passages in my Bible; it's clear that Solomon—and the Lord—are in favor of joyful and abundant living.

How, and why, are you able to enjoy life when there is so much suffering in the world?

_____

_____

_____

_____

_____

Warren Wiersbe has said that laughter is medicine for a broken heart, but sorrow is a hearty meal for the soul.

Reflect on two times in your life when both laughter and sorrow have been the right thing at the right time:

_____

_____

_____

_____

The word "name" in Hebrew is *shem*, and the word "ointment" in Hebrew is *shemen*. So Solomon is saying a shem is better than a sheman. . . . There are two days in our lives when our name is prominent: the day we receive our name at birth, and the day our name appears in the obituary column. What happens between those two determines whether our name is a lovely ointment, a *shemen,* or a foul stench.

To which are you giving the most attention in life: cultivating the shem *or the* shemen?

_____

_____

_____

_____

As a result of looking back to his grandfather's honorable life and standing on the name he had established in his community, Bill Bright was able to accomplish what he needed to do. That's an example of what Solomon means when he says, "A good name is better than precious ointment, and the day of death than the day of one's birth."

Recall a time when someone's good name—perhaps your own—was instrumental in meeting a goal:

_____

_____

_____

_____

Solomon was suggesting that if you die with a good name, you can no longer do anything to tarnish it. But on the day of your birth, you have an entire life before you yet unwritten. In that respect, if you have a good reputation, the day of your death is better than the day of your birth. Looking back on a life well lived is better than looking forward to a life unlived. Ending a good life is better than beginning an unknown life.

If you had to decide today on an epitaph for your gravestone, what would it be?

_____

_____

_____

_____

Sometimes even bombs are blessings. They fall from heaven, make a lot of noise, and liberate something wonderful within us—streams of living water that refresh us and draw us closer to Christ.

Recount a time when a "bomb" became a blessing in your life:

_____
_____
_____
_____
_____
_____

We are beginning to see the light. The highest purpose of life is *not* happiness.

How does that idea sit with you? If not happiness, what do you think is the highest purpose in life, and how does happiness relate to it?

_____
_____
_____
_____
_____
_____

We will realize that, until now, we never knew what happiness was—and never could have enjoyed it so richly now without the sorrow that was preparing our hearts all along the path.

How would you explain this concept to a spiritually immature person to whom the whole idea seems preposterous—that we only find true happiness in the wake of sorrow?

_____
_____
_____
_____
_____
_____
_____
_____

CHECKING YOUR PROGRESS

Contrast your highest purpose in life before knowing Christ with your highest purpose now in your walk with Him:

_____

_____

_____

_____

_____

ASKING FOR DIRECTIONS

In the spirit of 1 Corinthians 10:31 ("Whether you eat or drink, or whatever you do, do all to the glory of God"), write a prayer to God expressing your desire for Him to be your highest pursuit and purpose in life:

_____

_____

_____

_____

_____

Day 18

THE PLEASURE OF REBUKE

DAILY READING: Ecclesiastes 7:5–6

KEY VERSE
It is better to hear the rebuke of the wise than for a man to hear the song of fools.
—Ecclesiastes 7:5

BIG IDEA
I'm starting to realize that rebukes are really compliments turned inside out, designed to mold and mature us in wonderful ways.—DAVID JEREMIAH

EXCURSION JOURNAL
Nobody loves a critic. But let's get beyond the feel-good factor. Life isn't always about feeling good. That second fellow has given me food for thought. It may not taste like ice cream, but it's probably good for me. And later on, after my bruised ego recovers, I'll find that advice not only humbling but helpful.

How long does it take your bruised ego to recover from a rebuke or piece of strong advice?

_____

_____

_____

_____

_____

You and I both know that caring people also work in an advisory capacity: spouses, associates, good friends. Most of us are sharp enough to sort out the malicious jabs from the wise guidance.

Are you that sharp? How discerning are you when it comes to separating malicious jabs from wise guidance? Examples?

_____

_____

_____

Gordon MacDonald said. . . . : "Most of life is lived in the routine, and [my professor] was right: The man or woman who learns to make peace with routine responsibilities and obligations will make the greatest contributions in the long run."

Cite some evidence in your life that you either have, or have not, made peace with the fact that "life is lived in the routine":

_____

_____

_____

_____

_____

If you needed to heat up something quickly instead of preparing a fire for slow cooking, you would throw thorn branches on the fire. Solomon uses this illustration to say that the praise of fools is *quick, hot, showy*—but gone quickly. It flames up, dies out, and you need something else to stoke the fire. The rebuke of a wise man, however, can change your life forever.

Is the praise you give more like crackly thorn branches or an aged oak log? Reflect on times you've been either/or, and the results:

_____

_____

_____

_____

_____

Left to our own devices, we're not very teachable. It often takes us the awkward struggle of the teenage years to learn how to handle criticism—and some of us never do, even then.

Compare your chronological age with your ability-to-handle-criticism age. Are the two ages the same? Are you growing up while you're growing old?

_____

_____

_____

_____

_____

Have you made it known to people who care about you that they are free to share a word of advice, correction, or even rebuke with you when necessary? . . . At the right time, tell your spouse, coworker, or friend that his or her feedback is valuable to you.

Describe the relationship you have with someone to whom you have given permission to give you his or her feedback:

_____

_____

_____

_____

Don't be enamored with the praise of people who don't really care about you. Be more interested in the rebuke of a wise person who really loves you. Listen carefully to that person's instruction.

Recount the last time you were rebuked by a wise person who really loves you. Would you like this to happen more, or less, often?

_____

_____

_____

_____

_____

Find a friend and trust him enough to tell you when you're doing something wrong.

Who is that friend in your life? Has the relationship just evolved, or did you ask this person to play a trusted role in your life? Paint a picture of that relationship:

_____

_____

_____

_____

_____

In his book, *Restoring Your Spiritual Passion*, Gordon MacDonald said: "The rebuke stung, and I lived with its pain for many days afterward. But I will always be thankful for that rebuke, painful as it was, because I hear those words every time I am about to embarrass myself with a needless comment about another person. That was a rebuke that forced me to grow."

Describe a rebuke that caused you to grow:

_____

_____

_____

_____

Not only *can* we afford to listen to advice, we *must*. Surround yourself with good people who will help you, advise you, guide you, and hold you accountable. Your life will be like a river fed by many streams. Such a river grows broader and stronger, pounding its way through rugged territory, rushing along joyfully on its way to the vast sea.

Name all the people who are surrounding you, and what each contributes: help, advice, guidance, accountability. In whose life do you play one of those roles?

_____

_____

_____

_____

_____

CHECKING YOUR PROGRESS
On a scale of 1 to 10 (10 being "very willing"), evaluate your willingness to receive rebuke and correction from God, a family member, a friend, a coworker, a stranger:

_____

_____

_____

_____

_____

ASKING FOR DIRECTIONS
Compose a prayer in your own words asking God for increased willingness to receive words of wisdom delivered by His messengers:

_____

_____

_____

_____

_____

Day 19

THE HARD WAY MADE EASY

DAILY READING: Ecclesiastes 7:7–9

KEY VERSE
Do not hasten in your spirit to be angry, for anger rests in the bosom of fools.
—Ecclesiastes 7:9

BIG IDEA
Our destination is heaven on earth, but to get there we have to walk through difficult terrain. But it is worth it, for the end of the journey is better than the beginning.—DAVID JEREMIAH

EXCURSION JOURNAL
The hard way is an investment. If you personally work to upgrade your home, rather than hiring workers, you invest what real estate agents call "sweat equity" in that house. The financial value increases, but not nearly as much as your sense of pride in the home. You've earned it. You've owned the betterment process.

Describe an experience you've had with "sweat equity" of any sort, and what you learned from taking the hard way:

_____

_____

_____

_____

_____

There is a saying, "Devil take the high road." But in fact, the devil takes the shortcut and wants us to do the same. He knows that if we can be persuaded to take the easy way, we have shortchanged ourselves. We have sold ourselves out in the name of convenience and opened the door to selling out everything else that is meaningful.

Recount what you learned from a time when you chose to take the easy way instead of the hard way:

_____

_____

_____

_____

Jesus knew it, too. His road led through a trial, beatings, and the most violent and painful death we can imagine. But the destination was an empty tomb, a glorious ascension, a seat at the right hand of the Father.

What are the implications for your life that Jesus never chose to take the easy way?

_____

_____

_____

_____

The hard way will always be tough; there are no shortcuts. But it's made just a bit easier when we stop to remember that God never fails, that all His endings are happy ones, and that every bruise leads to deeper blessings.

Recount a time when a serious bruise in your life resulted in a deeper blessing than you imagined at the time:

_____

_____

_____

_____

Stephen Covey says we should begin with the end in mind. Covey suggests that we isolate where we want to end up, then keep that as an image that frames the way we think and act on a daily basis.

Cite a couple of areas of your life where you implement this principle as a practical matter: beginning with the end in mind.

_____

_____

_____

C. S. Lewis said, "The safest road to hell is the gradual one—the gentle slope, soft underfoot, without sudden turnings, without milestones, without signposts." It all begins with the little compromises, the "so what, no big deal" moments.

Create a warning to yourself about a "gentle slope" that you could easily start down if you are not careful:

_____

_____

_____

_____

My wife, Donna, and I have been married for forty-one years, and I can honestly say it gets better every year. . . . She is the one person in the world who is committed to loving me in spite of my many imperfections. Marriage done right gets better over time, because the end of a thing is better than the beginning.

How would you measure your own marriage (or other significant relationship)? Note how and why it is, or is not, getting better the further you go:

_____

_____

_____

_____

_____

CHECKING YOUR PROGRESS
How has your perception of difficulties changed over the years? Are they more friend or foe?

_____

_____

_____

_____

ASKING FOR DIRECTIONS
Romans 8:18 says that "the sufferings of this present time are not worthy to be compared with the glory" which is to come. In that spirit, compose a prayer of thanks to God that the end is indeed better than the beginning.

_____

_____

_____

_____

_____

Day 20

TIME TO MOVE ON

KEY VERSE

Do not say, "Why were the former days better than these?" For you do not inquire wisely concerning this."—Ecclesiastes 7:10

BIG IDEA

Today is the only day we can directly make an impact, and all our hopes of a better life lie right there in the calendar box where you stand—the day marked "Today."—DAVID JEREMIAH

EXCURSION JOURNAL

Can we agree that life is better in some ways and not nearly as good in others?

Jot down some ways in which the "good old days" were indeed better, and some ways in which they weren't—and some reasons why it doesn't matter either way:

_____

_____

_____

_____

Today never seems like anything special to the people inhabiting it. Today is always just short of yesterday's glory, just shy of tomorrow's promise. But today is all we have.

Why does that last statement—"But today is all we have"—seem somehow stark and bare? Is it an indication that we live too much in fantasy and not enough in reality?

_____

_____

_____

_____

When you talk about the past, you're not speaking from a position of careful rationality, comparing and contrasting all the microdifferences between eras (that would be impossible). You're speaking purely from emotions: feelings of fear, a sense of loss from yesterday, an insecurity about the future.

Are you a person who lives in and longs for the past? If so, why? If not, what is your focus, and how did you arrive at it?

_____

_____

_____

_____

_____

The issue in life is not your times, your trade, or your take-home pay. It's all about the question, *what are you doing with today?* Are you electrically charged with the prospect of all that God can do with your life in this window called Today?

Describe the degree to which the busyness of your life crowds out the opportunity to make something special of today? What should you do about that reality?

_____

_____

_____

_____

_____

The idea of heaven on earth is a Today idea. Remember how the Israelites took three steps toward the Promised Land, then two steps backward into nostalgia? Slavery never seemed so enticing.

Write down the specific things that represent your two steps back (or one, or three) to the past. Do you want to be free of those things? Why or why not?

_____

_____

_____

_____

_____

Heaven on earth has nothing of the past mixed in it, nor of what lies ahead. The heaven awaiting us, when we come face to face with our Savior, will be an eternal Now, and it stands to reason that the way to bring that heaven to earth is to live in *this* Now completely and consistently.

Use a scale of 1 to 10 (10 = completely and consistently) to indicate the degree to which you live in this Now. Why is your score what it is?

The truth is that it's not the kingdom of God that is upside down—it's the world. It's not the Word of God that turns life inside out—it's the world that has reversed all the equations that God designed for our lives.

Note some ways in which you see the world turning life inside out—making black out of white and down out of up. How often do you find yourself thinking like the world?

First, I *know* that "the whole creation groans and labors with birth pangs together until now" (Romans 8:22).

You are part of creation. In what ways do you groan and labor?

Second, I *don't know* what I should pray for as I ought, but "the Spirit Himself makes intercession for me with groanings which cannot be uttered" (Romans 8:26).

How dependent are you on the Holy Spirit to empower your prayer life this way?

And third, I *know* that "all things work together for good to those who love God, to those who are called according to His purpose" (Romans 8:28).

Recall the most recent way in which God caused all things to work together for good in your life:

_____

_____

_____

_____

_____

CHECKING YOUR PROGRESS

Describe how you stand today: straight up in the reality of today; leaning back, tied to yesterday; leaning forward, wanting to leap from today to tomorrow. Compare your stance today with how you stood five, ten, or fifteen years ago:

_____

_____

_____

_____

_____

_____

_____

_____

ASKING FOR DIRECTIONS

Compose a prayer asking God for eyes to see and ears to hear exactly what He has for you to do TODAY—*and grace to do it:*

_____

_____

_____

_____

_____

_____

Day 21

THE PERSPECTIVE OF WISDOM

DAILY READING: Ecclesiastes 7:11–18

KEY VERSE
In the day of prosperity be joyful, but in the day of adversity consider: Surely God has appointed the one as well as the other, so that man can find out nothing that will come after him.—Ecclesiastes 7:14

BIG IDEA
Wisdom is knowing how much we can't know, how small a piece of the puzzle we actually hold, and that while we know little, God knows all.
—DAVID JEREMIAH

EXCURSION JOURNAL
Wisdom may not solve all our problems or smooth out all the bumps in the road, but it gives the mind the right information for controlling the emotions.

Describe the daily (or at least, consistent) disciplines you engage in to keep your mind filled with "the right information" leading to wisdom:

_____

_____

_____

_____

_____

The work of God's perspective is similar. We look at the scene and see only random swirls of events until we fix our gaze on Christ, who is at the center of creation and holds all things together (Ephesians 1:10). As we step slowly back, we see the picture through new eyes.

What do you see when you look at the world, or circumstances in your own life? Do you see only the "random swirls of events," or are you able to see Jesus? How hard do you have to work to see Him?

_____

_____

_____

_____

Solomon tells us that wisdom and wealth make good companions. The Living Bible says, "To be wise is as good as being rich; in fact, it is better. You can get anything by either wisdom or money, but being wise has many advantages" (Ecclesiastes 7:11–12).

Are wisdom and wealth mutually exclusive, or can you have them both? Which do you have more of?

_____

_____

_____

_____

_____

Rich people who lack wisdom end up miserable; their wealth becomes a curse instead of a blessing. Wisdom gives perspective to prosperity. Wisdom keeps wealth in perspective.

Cite an example of wealth without wisdom and an example of wealth with wisdom. What do you learn from each?

_____

_____

_____

_____

_____

Worldwatch Institute reports: "Only about a third of Americans report being very happy, the same as in 1957 when Americans were only half as wealthy.

What does this statistic suggest to you about the power of wealth to make people happy? How does it impact your own plans or desires?

_____

_____

_____

_____

_____

You may be trying to fill in a certain picture with your life, such as the picture of yourself as an entrepreneur who owns his own business; or yourself as courting and marrying a certain candidate. God may be (and usually is) filling in a completely different picture, a vaster and more comprehensive one involving any number of people and having implications that might be played out in coming centuries.

Describe the difference, if any, between the picture you are trying to fill in for your life and the picture God seems to be filling in. Are you comfortable with whatever difference you see?

_____

_____

_____

_____

When good things happen, we never ask why God allowed them. Apparently we figure we have them coming!

Recall the most recent good thing that happened to you. How do you explain it?

_____

_____

_____

_____

Blessings in the hand plus burden on the back equals balance in the spiritual life—a formula for contentment and maturity.

Do you feel balanced or out of balance at this point in your life? Explain:

_____

_____

_____

_____

In the puzzle of life, we are often able to work out the borders of things—the places where life is straight, where its corners meet neatly. But to solve the big picture, we need wisdom, persistence, and perhaps the help of loved ones.

How puzzled are you by the puzzle of life? How much time do you spend talking with others, seeking counsel, and praying about the pieces of the puzzle which don't seem to fit?

_____

_____

_____

_____

CHECKING YOUR PROGRESS

Identify the puzzle piece in your life that seems more out of place than any other—a piece which doesn't connect with any other pieces at all:

_____
_____
_____
_____
_____

ASKING FOR DIRECTIONS

Write out a prayer specifically about that piece of your life, asking God to show you where and how it fits—and to give you patience until it does:

_____
_____
_____
_____
_____

Day 22

THE POWER OF WISDOM

DAILY READING: Ecclesiastes 7:19–20

KEY VERSE
Wisdom strengthens the wise more than ten rulers of the city.
—Ecclesiastes 7:19

BIG IDEA
When we apply *hokmah* (Hebrew for "wisdom") to the everyday course of human events, we could say that a wise person is one who possesses the skill of living. We would be those who know how to bring order out of a sometimes chaotic life, who can gather up life's random bits and pieces and shape them into something that bears fruit, and who can keep from crashing on the shallows and shoals of life and make it safely to port.—DAVID JEREMIAH

EXCURSION JOURNAL
These three young men were not afraid of the problem they faced. Wisdom told them that God's plan, not Nebuchadnezzar's, would ultimately prevail.

What skill did Shadrach, Meshach, and Abednego possess? How much of that skill do you recognize in yourself?

_____

_____

_____

_____

Listening to [negative] input isn't wise since it only serves to cause internal agitation when we hear it.

How skillful are you in turning off communication that serves only to harm? Which is a higher value for you: curiosity or caution?

_____

_____

_____

_____

What Solomon means by his counsel is this: "Let's be honest. If we get upset when people talk about us, we are holding them to a higher standard than we hold ourselves to, because we are prone to do the same thing."

How prone are you to "do the same thing"? Consider your skills in keeping hurtful communication to yourself:

_____

_____

_____

_____

_____

When I was growing up, I would often hear this phrase: "I don't know about the future, but I know who holds the future."

What degree of comfort does this phrase hold for you? How much skill is there in who you know as opposed to what you know?

_____

_____

_____

_____

_____

There is power in not being a slave to knowing why everything in life happens as it does, a power that comes from freedom. Many a martyr's body has been shackled into submission while his spirit remained free. That is true power, and it comes from the wisdom of God.

If there is power in freedom from needing to know everything, how powerful are you? How powerful is a person who is a slave to his or her fears?

_____

_____

_____

_____

_____

In Proverbs 2:1–10 Solomon talks about acquiring wisdom by listening to instruction, asking for it, searching for it like buried treasure.

Make some notes on the nature of searching for buried treasure. How hard is it? How often do you find it? How much of a prospector for wisdom are you?

_____

_____

_____

_____

Who wouldn't be attracted to the person James describes?

If people are attracted to what is scarce (for example, gold), what does that say about the amount of wisdom in our world? About the amount of the skill of living in your life?

_____

_____

_____

_____

The least of the saints has more wisdom in Christ than the most ingenious scientist possesses without Christ.

To what degree is intelligence made a priority in our culture? To what degree have you chosen to make wisdom, rather than intelligence, a priority in your life?

_____

_____

_____

_____

CHECKING YOUR PROGRESS
What are you more skillful at doing now than you were a few years ago? What price did you pay to acquire your skills?

_____

_____

_____

_____

ASKING FOR DIRECTIONS
In a prayer of your own making, ask the Lord for more skill . . . deeper skill . . . greater skill . . . Christlike skill for avoiding the shoals and shallows of life:

_____

_____

_____

_____

Day 23

HARD TO BE HUMBLE

DAILY READING: Ecclesiastes 8:1–17

KEY VERSE
When I applied my heart to know wisdom and to see the business that is done on earth, even though one sees no sleep day or night, then I saw all the work of God, that a man cannot find out the work that is done under the sun. For though a man labors to discover it, yet he will not find it; moreover, though a wise man attempts to know it, he will not be able to find it.
—Ecclesiastes 8:16–17

BIG IDEA
Humility puts us in our proper place; it strips away the coat of pride that collects on our surface as we travel through life's more successful moments.
—DAVID JEREMIAH

EXCURSION JOURNAL
A man who is truly wise is changed by the wisdom of God; even his countenance reflects his humility.

What are your thoughts about the connection between wisdom and countenance?

_____

_____

_____

_____

_____

William L. Stridger wrote, "A person's face is the signature of his soul."

Reflect on the signature that you have seen in various faces. Then think about the signature your own countenance offers to those who see you:

_____

_____

_____

_____

We must submit to bosses we don't always respect. We must study textbooks whose assumptions we question. The church may make a decision or two that doesn't set well with us. At what point do we quit the job or leave the church? It's hard to know; we feel humbled, and we move closer to God for guidance. There is much we can't change, and that we simply trust to Him.

Consider some recent decisions that have affected you, and your response. Did you draw nearer to God or move further away?

_____

_____

_____

_____

Impotent anger fills us when others control our lives. But in situations we can't change, the only healthy response is humility. Though it may sound trite or ineffectual, we must leave it all to God, knowing He will care for us.

Are you a control freak? Do you live or work with one? Why is "leave it all to God" not a trite statement when it comes to control?

_____

_____

_____

_____

We're a country of control freaks. The whole message of our society is to be independent, to take control of everything, to be your own boss. But God didn't design us that way.

Why do you think we (you) are so intent on controlling our own lives? Where does that impulse come from? What are the positive and negative aspects (in your life) of this tendency?

_____

_____

_____

_____

_____

In *Prodigals and Those Who Love Them*, Ruth Bell Graham writes: "We mothers must take care of the possible and trust God for the impossible. We are to love, affirm, encourage, teach, listen to, and care for the physical needs of the family. We cannot convict of sin, create hunger and thirst after God, or convert. These are miracles, and miracles are not in our department."

If you are a parent, how well have you learned this lesson? What circumstances helped you conclude that you couldn't control your children's spiritual lives?

_____

_____

_____

_____

We must trust God with what we can't control. That includes those who want to hurt or distress us—along with all the other unavoidable, unalterable troubles of life.

Consider three areas of your life you can control at present, and three you can't. Toward which list are you investing the most energy and resources?

_____

_____

_____

_____

If someone gets more praise than they deserve, let them, for it's little enough reward in the big picture, and they still have to stand before God. If you see someone receiving too little praise, take the initiative and call a celebration. But know that this one, too, will stand before God and receive his or her crown of glory.

Consider your experiences with both kinds of praise: undeserved but given, deserved but withheld. How did you handle both, and with how much humility?

_____

_____

_____

_____

We don't see God sending the lightning bolt upon the neighborhood hedonist, so we assume He's asleep at the wheel. He is not. There will be a reckoning for all who have strayed between the cradle and the crypt.

Note a situation where you believe "lightning bolts" would be appropriate. Are you seething in anger, or submitting in humility toward God's lack of action?

_____

_____

_____

_____

_____

The secret of life, the power of finding heaven on earth, is embracing heaven while accepting earth. We change what we can, we accept what we can't, and we walk on with the joy of God's companionship.

Evaluate your life in light of the above "secret of life." Where do changes need to be made?

_____

_____

_____

_____

_____

CHECKING YOUR PROGRESS

Compare the victories with the defeats in your life in recent years. Has humility tracked with the highs and lows, or has it found an increasingly constant track to run on?

_____

_____

_____

_____

_____

ASKING FOR DIRECTIONS

Compose a prayer in which you ask God to do whatever it takes to teach you to be humble . . . to trust Him with what you don't understand:

_____

_____

_____

_____

_____

Day 24

Dropping the "D" Word

Daily Reading: Ecclesiastes 9:1–10

Key Verse
Whatever your hand finds to do, do it with your might; for there is no work or device or knowledge or wisdom in the grave where you are going.—Ecclesiastes 9:10

Big Idea
Once again, this is heaven on earth; paradise in our hands; delivery from dread and drudgery, for this is the day the Lord has made, and we can rejoice and be glad in it.—David Jeremiah

Excursion Journal
So whether we lean to the reverent right or the flippant left, we lean away from speaking directly of the ultimate enemy.

How comfortable are you with death? What is the source of your emotions on the subject?

_____
_____
_____
_____

But for all of us who ride on spaceship earth, the end is imminent. Every human being lives out a death sentence.

How prepared are you to die? Do you welcome or dread the event? Why?

_____
_____
_____
_____

Death is the cousin everyone shares and no one has met; we only know he will get around to see every relative sooner or later. Are you squirming yet? Stay with me—it's not morbid to discuss what is so inevitable, so universal, and so profoundly important to the soul.

If you are a Christian, why should you have no hesitancy in discussing—or welcoming—death?

_____

_____

_____

_____

In *None of These Diseases*, Dr. David E. Stern relates the contrast of the two rooms: "One, a terrified man dropping into the unknown. The other, a restful soul passing through heaven's gate." How then shall we face death?

If you could choose the time and setting of your own death, describe what you would see:

_____

_____

_____

_____

Hope is only valid when it's reality-based—and our hope is on the ultimate reality.

What is the ultimate reality that lies behind your own feelings about death?

_____

_____

_____

_____

_____

Solomon's message is, if you like ice cream, have a second helping while you can. If you enjoy travel, see the world as soon as possible. You know the number of minutes in an hour and the number of hours in a day, but you do not know the number of days in a lifetime. There could be seven more, or seven thousand.

How do you handle the tension between knowing and not knowing, between saving for the future and enjoying life today?

_____

_____

_____

_____

We're surprised to see how many verses in the Bible tell us to simply enjoy our meals. In the Jewish culture, the meal was a very important time. Today we hardly eat a meal together at all. We share a meal with the television, or eat on the run as we drive. We've lost the ancient art and pleasure of the shared meal.

Describe the role meals play in your hierarchy of values (not the food itself as much as the event). Do your practices regarding meals reflect your values? Explain.

_____

_____

_____

_____

_____

Exactly! That's a great reason to let every waking moment be a celebration of God's gift of life. Get dressed. Eat out with a friend. Why? Because you can! And because God enjoys your enjoyment.

How convinced are you that God enjoys your enjoyment? How much of a role does enjoyment— "because you can!"—play in your life?

_____

_____

_____

_____

_____

There are moments of irritation and seasons of discontent, but remember those are days and seasons we have but one. Why not let each day be as joyful as your honeymoon? Marital fulfillment is a choice; choose to live and love joyfully.

If you are married, how much of your marriage is a result of your conscious choices to redeem each day—not to allow days of discontent to become seasons of discontent?

_____

_____

_____

_____

_____

Now imagine someone rising in the morning to say, "Thank you, Lord! Another day to use the gifts and the strength and the mind You have given me—to apply them to fruitful enterprise. What a gift you have given me, that I may work and serve."

To what degree are the above words an echo of your own words morning by morning? Do you see each day as a gift or a sentence?

_____

_____

_____

_____

_____

CHECKING YOUR PROGRESS
If a stranger followed you around for a month and submitted a report on the degree to which you appear to enjoy life, what do you think it would say?

_____

_____

_____

_____

ASKING FOR DIRECTIONS
Take Jesus at His word ("I have come that they may have life, and that they may have it more abundantly.") Write a prayer of thanks to God for the opportunity to live an abundant life—and for boldness to do so:

_____

_____

_____

_____

_____

Day 25

LIFE CHEATS!

DAILY READING: Ecclesiastes 9:11–18

KEY VERSE
Words of the wise, spoken quietly, should be heard rather than the shout of a ruler of fools.
—Ecclesiastes 9:17

BIG IDEA
Life is unfair and death is unstoppable, but we have what we have, and it happens to be this day before us—a gift from God, filled with pleasures, with beauty, with the satisfying enterprise of work and the precious presence of God, overseeing it all.—DAVID JEREMIAH

EXCURSION JOURNAL
No one likes cruel technicalities, but rules are rules.

We break rules because we think they're unfair. How are you with rules? Do you keep them, or are you willing to fudge when you think it's more fair?

_____

_____

_____

_____

_____

Life isn't fair. The race isn't always to the swift.

Recall a time in your life when you felt you were unfairly treated. What was your response? What did you learn?

_____

_____

_____

_____

Things are *supposed* to be fair, aren't they? Everyone would agree that life—and the people in it—should play by the rules.

What do you say to your children—or anyone—when they say, "That's not fair"? Why would a righteous God allow such unfairness?

_____

_____

_____

_____

_____

The race isn't always to the swift, nor the quarterback position to the best arm. "Learn it now when you're young," I told my son Daniel, "lest you learn it much more painfully down the road."

What have you learned about life's fairness the older you get? Does it get any more fair, or not? What must change, therefore, you or life?

_____

_____

_____

_____

_____

Solomon says, "Get used to it. Life takes what you have to give, forgets all about you, and moves on." You may try to have a biblical perspective on death by being realistic and responding to it by focusing on life—and then life sticks it to you!

Have your efforts to play by the rules been rewarded with a fair shake in life? No? Then why continue playing by the rules? (What's your answer?)

_____

_____

_____

_____

_____

C. S. Lewis put it this way: "God has provided many inns for us along life's journey, but He's made dead sure that we never confuse any of them for home."

What does life's unfairness keep you longing for? How anxious are you to reach your ultimate home?

_____

_____

_____

_____

When God's heartbreaking goodness intersects with human barbarity, the lights of heaven break through the trees. For just a moment, the intense darkness flees in the presence of that eternal light. All the unfairness and injustice is momentarily forgotten in the face of the obvious truth that our God is near, He is in control, and He will make all things right.

Can you recall a time in your personal experience when God's goodness broke through a situation of unfairness and provided a redemptive moment in spite of appearances? Were your feelings different after that happened than before? Should they have been?

_____

_____

_____

_____

_____

_____

CHECKING YOUR PROGRESS
What is the most unfair thing that has happened to you as an adult follower of Christ?

_____

_____

_____

_____

ASKING FOR DIRECTIONS
Compose a prayer based on the event above, thanking God for it and asking Him for fresh insight into His perfect and eternal rightness.

_____

_____

_____

_____

Day 26

FOOLISHNESS IN LITTLE THINGS

DAILY READING: Ecclesiastes 10:1–3

KEY VERSE
*A wise man's heart is at his right hand, but a fool's heart
at his left.*—Ecclesiastes 10:2

BIG IDEA
A fool is traditionally a comic figure, but foolishness can be as serious as
wildfire.—DAVID JEREMIAH

EXCURSION JOURNAL
To illustrate his point that little things can create big problems, Solomon uses a
rather unusual illustration about perfume.

*Can you recall an instance when a little thing created a big problem in your life? What did you
learn from that experience?*

_____

_____

_____

_____

It's Solomon's vivid way of illustrating how a tiny bit of foolishness can destroy
the powerful fragrance of a person's dignity and reputation.

*Have you, or someone you observed, lost their dignity or reputation because of an indiscretion?
What does it take to restore what was lost?*

_____

_____

_____

Over and over, giants are slain by the details.

Are you a detail person? How willing are you to become one for the sake of avoiding foolishness?

_____

_____

_____

_____

_____

"No big deal," we think, "just a little thing." A "little" relationship, a "little" flirtation at the office," a "little" edge in the tone of voice, a "little" padding on the expense account, a "little" experimentation in the wrong area—*just a little thing.*

What "little" details are there in your life that could erupt into big deals? Do they need your attention now?

_____

_____

_____

_____

_____

Obedience in little things implies that we're standing in a place of wisdom and power. When we keep slipping up in little things, it indicates we're standing in a place of foolishness and our power and influence are diluted.

Think about your family . . . your job . . . your personal affairs. Where are you standing at present? How might you stand differently with a reaffirmation to the little things?

_____

_____

_____

_____

_____

If Jesus had yielded to the lure of the little thing at that moment, all that followed would have been impossible. The spotless Lamb could not have been slain; the atonement could not have been achieved; the sin could not have been forgiven; and you and I would be without any hope for this life or the one to come.

Consider whether your yielding to a little thing is any less significant than Jesus's yielding to a little thing? Should you take the challenge any less seriously because you're not the Son of God?

_____

_____

_____

What about your life? What are the little horseshoe nails, the little crusts of bread, the tiny tempters that affect the direction of your life? According to Solomon, the one who pays the terrible price for the tiny bait is the fool.

Write them down—all the little things you're being lax about. Why is the comfort of avoidance worth the shame of failure?

_____

_____

_____

_____

_____

Ask God, through the loving grace and overcoming power of His Holy Spirit, to afford you the wisdom to choose light at every turn. I believe that as you connect the dots of wise choices, a great haze will drop away from your vision.

CHECKING YOUR PROGRESS
What is the detail that could have the most dramatic negative ramifications in your life if not attended to?

_____

_____

_____

_____

ASKING FOR DIRECTIONS
In the spirit of Philippians 4:6 ("Let your requests be made known to God"), write out a prayer asking God for grace to attend to the detail you mentioned above, that wisdom might attend your way:

_____

_____

_____

_____

Day 27

FOOLISHNESS IN LEADERSHIP

DAILY READING: Ecclesiastes 10:4–7, 16–19

KEY VERSE
Blessed are you, O land, when your king is the son of nobles, and your princes feast at the proper time—for strength and not for drunkenness!—Ecclesiastes 10:17

BIG IDEA
Remember that a good leader walks ahead of his people, to point the way; beside his people, to share in their journey; and behind his people, to protect them and cover their mistakes.—DAVID JEREMIAH

EXCURSION JOURNAL
When we see a boss or a leader of any kind abuse power, our first impulse is to just walk away. But Solomon says there's a better way still. Don't panic; don't quit your job; and don't leave your post. Don't overreact to an overreaction. Just hang in there and deal with the person.

What is your first impulse when you are the recipient of an abuse of power by a leader? What would you like your first impulse to be?

_____

_____

_____

_____

_____

There is little to be gained in hating another person, President Dwight Eisenhower's mother told him as she put salve on his injured hands. We only hurt ourselves.

Describe a time when your ill feelings toward another only ended in harm to yourself—and what you learned:

_____

_____

_____

_____

_____

In his book *At Ease: Stories I Tell to Friends,* Eisenhower tells how whenever someone angered him, he would write the person's name on a piece of scrap paper, drop it into the lowest drawer in his desk, and say to himself, "That finishes the incident."

Have you developed a method for "finishing the incident"? Practically and spiritually, what do you do?

_____

_____

_____

_____

Robert Greenleaf says servant-leaders may or may not be in formal positions of leadership. That means anyone can be a servant-leader.

Since we are all part of Greenleaf's "anyone," who are the people you lead? How challenging do you find being a servant-leader?

_____

_____

_____

_____

One of America's foremost leadership gurus, Peter Drucker, once observed there is little correlation between a leader's effectiveness and his or her intelligence, imagination, or knowledge. Brilliant people are often strikingly ineffectual, he said. "They have never learned that insights become effectiveness only through hard systematic work."

How would you apply Drucker's comment to your own life? How much hard systematic work do you find it takes to serve those you lead?

_____

_____

_____

_____

Do you know how to identify the mature leaders? They're the ones who take the blame when things go wrong but share the credit when things go well.

Reflect on the degree to which this statement characterizes you—or not:

_____
_____
_____
_____
_____
_____

How does God view laziness? Take your Bible sometime and read through Proverbs, underlining the verses that talk about being slothful, lazy, diligent, or hardworking. You'll come away with a whole new perspective on ambition and energy in your life.

How tired do you get of the constant need to inject energy (work) into the daily processes of life? How reconciled are you to that being the way life is this side of heaven?

_____
_____
_____
_____
_____
_____

In what field of life are you a leader? In the home? At work? In a Sunday school class? If you're wise, you'll realize that you never stand alone before God; with you stand the souls of those you lead. Your stewardship of these souls is an issue with eternal consequences—a heaven on earth issue.

You are a steward; those you lead are your responsibility to "manage." So who are you managing them for? Who is the overseer for whom you work as a steward? How does the answer to that question impact your role as a steward-leader?

_____
_____
_____
_____
_____

CHECKING YOUR PROGRESS

Reflect on your skills (wisdom) as one who walks ahead of, alongside, and behind those you lead. What would you like to do in a more servantlike manner?

_____

_____

_____

_____

_____

ASKING FOR DIRECTIONS

Using Jesus as a model ("The Son of Man did not come to be served, but to serve"), compose a prayer asking God for a servant's heart toward those you lead:

_____

_____

_____

_____

_____

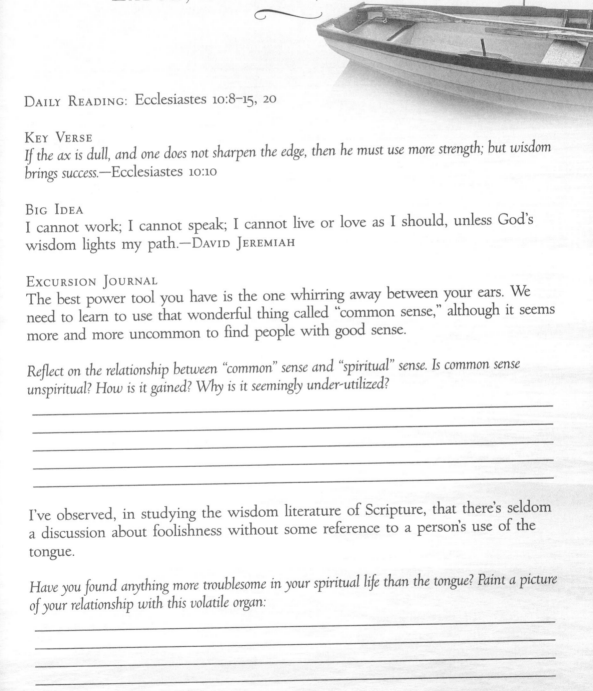

Day 28

LABOR, LANGUAGE, AND LUNACY

DAILY READING: Ecclesiastes 10:8–15, 20

KEY VERSE
If the ax is dull, and one does not sharpen the edge, then he must use more strength; but wisdom brings success.—Ecclesiastes 10:10

BIG IDEA
I cannot work; I cannot speak; I cannot live or love as I should, unless God's wisdom lights my path.—DAVID JEREMIAH

EXCURSION JOURNAL
The best power tool you have is the one whirring away between your ears. We need to learn to use that wonderful thing called "common sense," although it seems more and more uncommon to find people with good sense.

Reflect on the relationship between "common" sense and "spiritual" sense. Is common sense unspiritual? How is it gained? Why is it seemingly under-utilized?

_____
_____
_____
_____

I've observed, in studying the wisdom literature of Scripture, that there's seldom a discussion about foolishness without some reference to a person's use of the tongue.

Have you found anything more troublesome in your spiritual life than the tongue? Paint a picture of your relationship with this volatile organ:

_____
_____
_____
_____

If there's one place where we can spot foolishness, it's in the way people use their tongues. Solomon shows us five ways misuse of the tongue reveals a foolish heart.

Make your own list of five ways the tongue is a challenge for you personally:

_____

_____

_____

_____

_____

In Ecclesiastes 3, Solomon says there is a time to speak and a time to be silent.

Reflect on your listening skills—why listening is easy or why it's hard. Why do you think listening is so hard for most people?

_____

_____

_____

_____

_____

Just between you and me, do you have a tendency to talk too much? Have you seen it in people's eyes during your conversations?

How would you answer that probing question? How do you know (based on others' reactions) when you're talking too much? How consistently do you heed the warning signs?

_____

_____

_____

_____

_____

_____

I'm sure you'll agree that some of the worst problems of your life have been instigated by your tongue—or someone else's.

Recount a couple of your worst—what you did and what you learned. Have there been fewer worst moments as you've matured?

_____
_____
_____
_____
_____

Solomon is reminding us with this illustration that a wise person doesn't say something in private that he wouldn't want someone to hear in public.

Has a "little bird" ever shared something you said that you didn't want repeated? Recall the experience and what you learned from it:

_____
_____
_____
_____
_____

CHECKING YOUR PROGRESS
What has given you the greatest satisfaction in terms of progress with your speech? What remains your biggest challenge?

_____
_____
_____
_____
_____

ASKING FOR DIRECTIONS
Write out a prayer of thanks to God for the times your speech is seasoned by grace (Colossians 4:6), and a petition that it might always be so:

_____
_____
_____
_____
_____

Day 29

LIFE IS UNCERTAIN: EMBRACE IT!

KEY VERSE
In the morning sow your seed, and in the evening do not withhold your hand; for you do not know which will prosper, either this or that, or whether both alike will be good.—Ecclesiastes 11:6

BIG IDEA
The Lord could come today or He could come in a thousand years. In either case, let us be about our Father's business.—DAVID JEREMIAH

EXCURSION JOURNAL
The Bible is a far better source of inspiration than paper towels or church signs, but as Solomon ends his book of Ecclesiastes his message is one the columnist would embrace—*life is uncertain.*

Reflect on the things in life that you know are certain (which assumes that everything you don't list is uncertain). How do you respond to so much uncertainty in your life?

_____

_____

_____

_____

In his vast wisdom, Solomon understands that life under the sun, without God, is a meaningless experience. It's life on the treadmill—you get your exercise, but you don't go anywhere.

Is that how you felt about life before knowing Christ? To what degree do you still experience the "treadmill" effect?

_____

_____

_____

Solomon's first point about life is that it's uncertain; therefore, it is to be embraced.

Describe the kind of person you are: one who embraces uncertainty or one who embraces certainty? Give examples.

_____
_____
_____
_____
_____
_____

Because men are evil, we do not know what will happen. People are evil, and that invites uncertainty into the world.

To what degree do you fear the evil that others might do to you? What is the difference between approaching life with fatalism and approaching it with faith?

_____
_____
_____
_____
_____
_____

Because God's plans are hidden, we do not know what will happen. He may call us home at any instant—or He may send us on some new earthly mission. God moves in mysterious ways, and that invites uncertainty into the world.

How much is God's "all knowingness" a comfort to you? Does it help that He knows the future even if you don't?

_____
_____
_____
_____
_____
_____

The world is a mystery and life but a vapor, Solomon tells us; but hard work, wise living, and joyful countenance are not. They are the best chance for those who would make the most of earth on their way to heaven. Life is uncertain—embrace it with joy.

If you saw a hard-working, wise-living, and joyful Christian and a non-Christian, how would you know which was which? How much of the Christian life is fairly mundane instead of super-spiritual?

_____
_____
_____
_____

In these days of uncertainty, we can ask for no better course. Even as the darkness falls, the light is certain to overcome it. So bring the candles. Lift them aloft to spread their light for as long as the wax holds out, for as long as our strength holds out.

How is your life a source of light in this dark world?

_____
_____
_____
_____
_____

CHECKING YOUR PROGRESS
Describe the way you integrate "being about the Father's business" with the uncertainty of life—and why it's a good use of your time, given that it could all be erased tomorrow:

_____
_____
_____
_____
_____

ASKING FOR DIRECTIONS
In light of Proverbs 16:9 ("A man's heart plans his way, but the LORD directs his steps"), compose a prayer asking God for discernment and wisdom in being about His business in spite of all that you do not and cannot know:

_____
_____
_____
_____
_____

Day 30

LIFE IS SHORT: ENJOY IT!

DAILY READING: Ecclesiastes 11:7–12:8

KEY VERSE
Remember now your Creator in the days of your youth, before the difficult days come, and the years draw near when you say, "I have no pleasure in them."—Ecclesiastes 12:1

BIG IDEA
We mustn't spend too much time brooding over life's transience, for that defeats the very purpose. A time is to be used, to be invested in joy and meaning.
—DAVID JEREMIAH

EXCURSION JOURNAL
I dare you to begin the next seven days with intense, heartfelt praise and worship. Read a praise psalm each day, and reflect on a thoughtful hymn. Praise Him for the sunshine or the rain—whichever blessing comes that day. Exalt Him for the sheer goodness of a life that features His presence. Sit at His feet for just a few moments, then watch the effect on your day.

What role does thanksgiving play in your daily routines? Consider taking the seven-day challenge and record the results:

_____

_____

_____

_____

_____

"What a pity," Sigmund Freud wrote, "that one has to grow old and ill before [discovering the glories of springtime]."

What parts of life have you discovered as you've grown older that you don't know how you missed when you were younger?

_____

_____

_____

I'm glad I can make this discovery anew every morning. Were you to peek inside my journal, you'd find that almost every entry says in one way or another: "Thank You, Lord, for this day, for a good night's rest, and for the privilege of being alive one more day on this earth to serve You."

Have you discovered the value of journaling? One way or another, how often does "Thank You, Lord" get written on the pages of your life?

_____

_____

_____

_____

_____

Robert Louis Stevenson said, "The person who has stopped being thankful has fallen asleep in life." Develop the attitude of totally experiencing each day.

Talk about the degree to which you experience each day totally—that is, you experience life in conscious and continual awareness of God's presence, gifts, and interventions:

_____

_____

_____

_____

_____

As I've watched the young people in my church and community, it seems that they're always eager to be two years older. Sixteen-year-olds want to be eighteen, and eighteen-year-olds can't wait to be twenty or twenty-one. Somewhere along the way that process starts to reverse itself!

Where are you in that process—looking forward or looking back? Or happy and content with your age today?

_____

_____

_____

_____

_____

While young people face many challenges and difficulties today, it's also true that life tends to become harder and heavier as we grow older. Solomon counsels us to rejoice in our youth.

What do you find that is becoming harder and heavier as you grow older? How do those experiences cause you to rejoice and make the most of each day?

_____

_____

_____

_____

If I were a new parent, I would let my kids be kids. I wouldn't want them to grow up too quickly, and when they stumble along the learning path, I would gently help them up and show them how to walk upright.

Think about this from your own youth or from the youthful years of your children: how many parents encourage their children to savor their youth instead of pushing them to grow up.

_____

_____

_____

_____

Solomon says, "_Now_ is the very time to draw near to your God. The longer you wait, the less you will desire Him, and the more elusive He will prove to be. _Now_ is the time when you will make the pivotal decisions on which your whole future will turn. Please don't make them without your Lord."

Did you hear that message when you were young? How did you respond? Do you say it to your children? What's the best way to reach children with a serious spiritual message?

_____

_____

_____

_____

Let's encourage our young people and pray for them. God's going to use them to change the world, and they need a head start. They need to remember their Creator in the days of their youth.

What are you doing to encourage your own (or other) children to seek the Lord? How difficult a challenge is it? How successful are you at it?

_____
_____
_____
_____
_____

CHECKING YOUR PROGRESS

Do you spend more time brooding over the transience of life or enjoying life? Which do you do more of the older you get?

_____
_____
_____
_____
_____

ASKING FOR DIRECTIONS

Compose a prayer in the spirit of Psalm 90:12: "So teach us to number our days, that we may gain a heart of wisdom."

_____
_____
_____
_____
_____

Day 31

LIFE IS MYSTERIOUS: EXAMINE IT!

DAILY READING: Ecclesiastes 12:9–12

KEY VERSE
The words of the wise are like goads, and the words of scholars are like well-driven nails, given by one Shepherd.—Ecclesiastes 12:11

BIG IDEA
We mustn't get so caught up in postmodern inquiry as to forget that questions are for answers, and the answers are available in God's Word.—DAVID JEREMIAH

EXCURSION JOURNAL
I prefer to say that wisdom is the ability to apply biblical truth to real-life situations. . . . It's the ability to perceive how the God of heaven sees a situation and to apply His divine wisdom to it.

Reflect on your own level of wisdom. That is, how competent do you feel to "apply biblical truth to real-life situations?"

_____

_____

_____

_____

_____

As we study the proverbs of Solomon, we'll grow in wisdom. And sometimes a simple sentence of truth—one Spirit-inspired sentence—can change a person's whole attitude and life.

Recall a proverb or two that have been especially meaningful, perhaps life-changing, for you:

_____

_____

_____

_____

Do you ever struggle to find just the right words to say to someone? Well, remember God's offer in James 1:5, "If any of you lacks wisdom, let him ask of God, who gives to all liberally and without reproach, and it will be given to him."

Is this verse part of your spiritual arsenal? Consider memorizing it, if you haven't already, and make it a ready prayer in any and every situation. Describe a current situation in which you could use God's wisdom:

_____

_____

_____

_____

_____

How often have I been in a crisis or tense situation and claimed this truth. I've been with my children, my parishioners, or with someone needing my help, and I've whispered a prayer to God: "Lord, give me wisdom!" If you've been abiding in the Scriptures, it's amazing and inspiring how just the right word rolls off your tongue.

Recall an experience in which you (1) needed wisdom, (2) prayed for it, and (3) it was provided:

_____

_____

_____

_____

_____

Ruth Graham was once asked the best way to become wise. Her reply, "Read, read, read—but use the Bible as home base."

Are you a reader? How does reading the Bible help you to be a more discerning reader of other material?

_____

_____

_____

_____

_____

To go through a day without immersing myself in the Bible's freshness would be like going through a day without bathing—or breathing, for that matter.

How do you respond to this statement? Does the Bible play such a central role in your life?

_____

_____

_____

_____

We often wonder whether those in the No-Absolutes camp—who claim one person's "truth" is as good as another's—really *want* to find the final Truth. If they could stand on the very borders of heaven, would they embrace the final answers, or turn and walk away to keep playing the game of Unending Speculation?

Which is more important to you: truth, or the pursuit of truth? In which do you find the most satisfaction?

_____

_____

_____

_____

_____

CHECKING YOUR PROGRESS
Survey the role the Bible has played in the course of your spiritual growth. How has your perspective of it and integration of it into your life changed over time?

_____

_____

_____

_____

ASKING FOR DIRECTIONS
Compose a prayer in the spirit of Psalm 119:18: "Open my eyes, that I may see wondrous things from Your law."

_____

_____

_____

_____

_____

CONCLUSION

DAILY READING: Ecclesiastes 12:13–14

KEY VERSE

Let us hear the conclusion of the whole matter: fear God and keep His commandments, for this is man's all. For God will bring every work into judgment, including every secret thing, whether good or evil.—Ecclesiastes 12:13–14

So much flashes before him: the world's great libraries; wise men from around the world; priests and princes and prophets; ships from exotic lands previously unknown. And all of it comes down to . . . *nothing.*

Write out the above paragraph using examples from your own life (house, cars, jobs, status—who you are and what you have). Are you comfortable with the idea that it all, in eternity's eyes, amounts to nothing?

_____

_____

_____

_____

And somehow this brief word trumps all the wisdom and learning of the world. And the word is this: Fear God, and keep His commandments, for this is man's all.

To what degree have you adopted Solomon's summation as your own creed by which to live?

_____

_____

_____

_____

For God will bring every work into judgment, including every secret thing, whether good or evil. You could have no riches, no power, no glory, none of life's ordinary pleasure, and if you knew that one thing—simple enough for any child—you would have the map to finding heaven on earth.

What kind of comfort and confidence do these words bring you as you navigate the shoals and swells of life?

_____

_____

_____

_____

_____

_____

Just beneath that, he scrawls, "KEEP HIS COMMANDMENTS!" Yes, Solomon nods, it is the only way. Find out what God wants done, and *go do it* regardless of the cost. All the rest is vanity; heartache; wandering blind.

In this postmodern age, where agreement on truth is rare, where is obedience to God on your value radar? Near the top? Close to the bottom? What does it mean to you that this is Solomon's final conclusion about life?

_____

_____

_____

_____

_____

_____

What has been the biggest benefit to you of studying Solomon's book of Ecclesiastes?

_____

_____

_____

_____

_____

_____

_____

Since there is nothing new under the sun, write out a final prayer to God asking Him for wisdom to learn from Solomon; to avoid making the same mistakes he did; to enjoy wisdom all your life instead of coming back to it at the end:

_____

_____

_____

_____

_____

_____